Praise for *How's the Culture in Your Kingdom?*

As a student of leadership in the U.S. Navy as well as the Walt Disney Company, I am impressed with how Dan has laid out his leadership lessons through engaging storytelling, thoughtful insights, and specific behavioral examples for readers to adopt.

Brian Britton
U.S.N.A. Class of 1989
CEO, National Heritage Academies

Dan's first writing effort, *How's the Culture in Your Kingdom?*, is an incredibly insightful and inspiring collection of experiences, offering insights and perspectives rarely found in typical books focused on leadership, management, and culture. The real-life lessons and learnings represent a rich collection of tools that can benefit every part of an organization.

Workplace culture should be at the core of each business. It is something more than a simple management objective. It has to be treated as a living, breathing thing… something that requires attention and constant feeding. What Dan has done is provide a highly relevant collection of management topics, each of which contributes to the building and sustainment of a vibrant workplace culture!

Congratulations and thank you for putting your Disney experiences to paper. This insightful treasure has to be a must-read for leaders.

Karl Holz
President (Retired)
Disney Cruise Line

How's the Culture in Your Kingdom?

How's the CULTURE in Your KINGDOM?

Lessons from a
Disney Leadership Journey

DAN COCKERELL
Former Vice President, Disney's Magic Kingdom

NEW YORK

LONDON • NASHVILLE • MELBOURNE • VANCOUVER

How's the Culture in Your Kingdom?

Lessons from a Disney Leadership Journey

Published in New York, New York, by Morgan James Publishing. Morgan James is a trademark of Morgan James, LLC. www.MorganJamesPublishing.com

ISBN 9781642798449 paperback
ISBN 9781642798456 eBook
Library of Congress Control Number: 2019951489

Cover & Interior Design by:
Christopher Kirk
www.GFSstudio.com

Morgan James is a proud partner of Habitat for Humanity Peninsula and Greater Williamsburg. Partners in building since 2006.

Get involved today! Visit
MorganJamesPublishing.com/giving-back

Dedication

Valerie
My love, my ghostwriter, my partner
Let's enjoy this ride!

Table of Contents

Foreword

uring my 41 years of service in the US Army, I led soldiers in both peacetime and in combat at every level. I can certainly recognize good leaders when I see them. Daniel Cockerell is not just a good leader.... He is a great one.

Having known Daniel for many years, I watched from afar as he climbed the leadership ladder at Disney with amazing speed. His success was not based solely on his charm, but rather his ability to apply good leadership principles and develop a productive climate in every organization that he led. This created a culture of excellence in each case.

In this book, Daniel Cockerell addresses the issue of building a culture of excellence in organizations. In doing so, he discusses the areas of Leading Self, Leading Team, Leading Organization, and Leading Change.

Daniel is a brilliant storyteller who uses personal experiences from his 26-year career with the Disney Corporation to illustrate key leadership lessons. It is superbly done.

He aptly takes key leadership principles and distills them down into plain language that can benefit leaders at all levels. His insights are absolutely relevant to any profession. Throughout the book, he is genuine, engaging, and effective.

Daniel goes beyond just providing thoughts on leadership theory. He provides concrete steps and recommended techniques that leaders can employ. It is something that leaders at all levels crave. While reading this book, I felt that I was having a conversation with a good friend... benefiting from his 26 years of lessons learned.

The leadership insights that Daniel shares in this book will benefit anyone who aspires to lead. Whether you are leading a military organization, a business unit, or a non-profit organization, you will definitely benefit from this book.

Lloyd J. Austin III, General, U.S. Army (Ret.)

Introduction

I n 2018, I stepped down from a twenty-six-year career at the Walt Disney Company. During the nearly three decades I spent at Disney, I held nineteen different positions, from parking attendant at Epcot to vice president of the Magic Kingdom in Orlando, Florida, the largest theme park in the world. At the Magic Kingdom, I led a team of 12,000 "cast members," the term Disney uses for employees—and a term that aptly reflects the collective commitment to creating a unique immersive show for all visitors.

Because I spent all of my professional life at Disney, the kingdom metaphor in the title of this book should come as no surprise. After all, we all operate in several "bubbles" or kingdoms of sorts: our personal life, our team, our organization. When I joined Disney in 1991, I knew very little about how to apply leadership in the real world or how to achieve success in a professional environment. Even with the best training in the industry, it took me a long time, many mistakes, and a lot of self-reflection to learn how to lead well and create the right culture. At first, I assumed leadership was all about what we did for our organizations. As the scope of my responsibilities grew, I realized that in order to have an effective and positive impact, I needed first to lead my direct reports well, hoping to steer them toward my goals for the organization.

Eventually, it became clear that none of this would happen if I, myself, wasn't fit to lead. Only then could I have the strength and ability to lead my team and subsequently impact the organization as a whole.

That single realization—*that self-leadership is paramount to team or organizational leadership*—was the most valuable lesson I learned in almost three decades at Disney. I structured my leadership training around that very lesson, helping all cast members turn into leaders by first leading themselves well.

Since leaving Disney, I've made it my mission to help leaders in other organizations do the same—lead themselves, their teams, and their organizations effectively, in that order—because the reality is the moment you start leading yourself well, your team and organization will begin to improve, too. As the speed of change reaches new heights, it requires us to be more malleable, adaptable, and innovative; this is akin to operating in transformation mode and constantly assessing how we can adapt to a new reality, be it economically, environmentally, or technologically.

Just like the impeccable housekeeping that cast members perform at Disney to deliver excellent guest experiences, we all need to do personal, internal housekeeping on ourselves to become impactful leaders in our personal and professional lives. It begins through a process of ongoing self-reflection, personal growth, and a commitment to self-discipline. This is true no matter which kingdom you lead.

Let the sun shine on your organization's culture.

With traditional management training, we measure productivity, revenue, cost, growth, and other key performance indicators, or KPIs. The truth is that these KPIs are simply results or lagging indicators of running a successful business. It is the people who deliver these results, and in order for them to perform at their best, they need to be in an environment where they feel supported and are encouraged along the way. This is where organizational culture comes in.

Culture is the all-encompassing environment within which we live, work, and play—it's the factor with the most influence on our mood, attitude, and motivation. You will see your KPIs improve faster as your team members become more engaged in their jobs. I like to equate culture with the weather. When the sun is shining and the weather is warm, it's easy to be positive, engaged, and committed. When it rains or snows, or when lightning strikes, everyone wants to run for cover. When we operate under auspicious skies in our organization, we are more motivated and energetic, more effective and fulfilled. The entire team can feel it—happy leader, happy team ... and a happy team makes an organization more dynamic, efficient, and successful.

During my tenure as the vice president of the Magic Kingdom, my team and I had to cope with many weather-related issues ranging from extreme heat and humidity to torrential downpours and sometimes even hurricanes. Each change in the weather shifted everything about the Magic Kingdom, from cast member duties to our guests' experience. There was no amount of pixie dust that could have influenced Mother Nature. On the other hand, I've learned that the weather in our personal and professional kingdoms is within our control. We can devise the ideal "weather" and the right environment for ourselves, our families, and our organizations. Not only do we have the ability to do something about it, but it is also our responsibility. In this book, I'm going to share with you exactly how I learned to influence culture in my kingdom.

What to Expect

I routinely coached and mentored leaders during my career at Disney, was coached and mentored myself, and knew I had to keep going beyond the Magic Kingdom walls. I spent more than two decades improving as a leader and serving others. Since I left Disney, one of my most rewarding professional experiences has been helping leaders become better equipped to serve others, empower their teams to higher performance, and build their organizations to be more successful. As Alexander Hamilton so eloquently said, "A legacy is planting seeds in a garden you never get to see." If, with this book, I can help leaders influence the culture in their kingdoms, I will leave a legacy far beyond what I imagined back in 1991, when I started at Disney.

I read somewhere that we should dedicate the first 25 years of our lives to learning, the following 25 years to doing, and the last 25 years to teaching. Well, I just turned 50 this year, so it looks like I am right on track. Sharing my experience and the lessons learned has been both exhilarating and gratifying.

Throughout the rest of this book, I will share what we must do as leaders at home and at work to become stronger and leave a legacy we will never get to see. I'm not talking about magical spells or pixie dust but rather the tools and insights I have personally tested with the various teams, big and small, I've led during my career.

These tools work well because they helped me improve and hone my focus. No leader can be everywhere at once. We have to prioritize our time, attention, tasks, strategies, goals, and even relationships.

I wrote this book for people who live in the real world, with real issues and real pulls on their time. I wrote it for busy leaders at work and home, breaking it down into four sections—leading self, leading others, leading organizations, and leading change. Within each of those parts, I share stories and practical takeaways as well as self-assessment tools and research-based best practices. At the end of each chapter, you will also find an action plan called "Fast Track to Results" to help you set priorities and improve in the most important areas of your life for the greatest chance at positive results and success.

In addition to discussing the necessary tools for leading self, team, organization, and change, I will help you prioritize the most important aspects of your life and keep those focuses strong. That way, you can better determine how you should spend your time, make better decisions, and know when to sacrifice one thing for something more important.

As leaders, it is within our control and our responsibility to create the right culture for our organizations. It is also the most important thing you can do for the success of those with whom you interact.

How to Use This Book

Life is busy. I get it. We have so many things pulling on our time. We hear thousands of conflicting messages about business and life every day. It's not easy to get motivated for something new, especially when we are unsure if it will work. It's hard to keep going when adversity strikes. And, let's face it, adversity *will strike*. At some point in time, we all struggle with lack of clarity, lack of time, lack of motivation, and even lack of self-discipline—I have overcome them all and helped thousands of other people navigate those challenges.

I anticipate that some people may not have a lot of extra time to read this book from cover to cover. If that's you, don't fear. I built the book to move quickly, with lessons that are easy to apply. You'll find quick wins and action steps to keep improving. If you read it from cover to cover, you will likely see that the themes build on each other. But you may also find that you need more help with some areas than others. Most of us have areas of strength and areas of "opportunity." The structure will help you see where you need to pay the most attention, and you will find the tools you need in the "Fast Track" section of each chapter.

What Success Looks Like

Before we move forward to the first part—Leading Self—I would like to take a minute to reflect on what success looks like in our world. As we have grown older, my wife and I have had many conversations about our lives. I've come to believe, from these conversations, that too many people allow others to define what their goals should be and what success looks like. Of course, social media has been a big contributor to this phenomenon. I used to struggle with this, too, comparing my situation to others' to determine whether I was "successful" or not. I'd do this everywhere. With social media, it is easy to see perfectly framed snapshots from other people's lives and decide that our lives should look exactly like that.

Looking back, I realize it makes no sense at all. Just outside of the most perfectly framed Instagram shot, chances are you'd find a crying baby, stressed spouse, or financial fiasco. The successful entrepreneur you admire may have zero quality of life. That runner you are trying to keep up with during a race may be struggling in many other ways or may have been training for years longer than you.

Determining *your* success based on the lives of *others* doesn't work. Even if you wanted to, you literally could not know enough about other people's lives to make an accurate comparison. So, my advice as you move forward with reading, reflecting, and taking action is to *run your own race*. Use the tools and insights as stepping stones to become a transformational leader and create the right culture for your kingdom. But only *you* get to decide what success looks like in your life; only *you* get to set your goals and decide when you have met those goals.

If all this talk about framework and leading *yourself first* is new to you, I understand. It can be hard to change after years or even decades of acting another way. Change is hard. Creating new habits is hard. I have attempted many new habits during the course of my life and have failed as many times as I have been successful. However, I have never stopped thinking about getting better, and I have never stopped trying to improve. Over time, that has helped me use my failures to fuel a better future.

As Rear Admiral Charles Norville Payne—my grandfather—wisely told me many years ago, "Do your best, and then forgive yourself." That is really all we can do. Let's get started!

Part 1:

LEADING SELF

As many military leaders would attest, surprise is a certainty in warfare. Even the best-laid plans can change or fail once we engage. No matter the scope of the battle, we can know and count on only so much. In anticipation of this surprise element, the best strategy is to increase our level of general preparedness. My grandfather often talked about his life on the USS *Columbia* during World War II. Every drill and every procedure mattered and could make the difference between life and death during a mission.

Likewise, leading a team and an organization requires a variety of competencies, a great deal of stamina, and preparation in anticipation of the surprise element. Yet we seldom acknowledge the fact that success can't happen if we aren't well prepared, or "fit to lead." This requires introspection, discipline, and commitment. Yet many of us wake up each morning to take on the day without asking ourselves the important questions:

- Am I well prepared?
- Am I giving myself the best chance to succeed?
- What does success look like?
- What will it take to get there?

We have not consciously thought about what makes us efficient and successful. We count on sheer brute force and improvisation to solve the most pressing and urgent issues before us. Meanwhile, we fail to make a dent in the list of things that actually matter. Somehow, we are never able to identify the root cause of our daily problems in order to generate solutions to make systemic improvements in our lives and make ourselves more effective leaders and happier people.

We need to take control of the most consequential areas of our lives. How easily we forget that the very forces that make us successful in life are the first ones that we sacrifice: physical, mental, and organizational fitness. When we ignore these, everything else becomes more difficult and more stressful. Fulfilling our responsibility with our family and our careers is hard enough. Why not stack the deck in our own favor and put ourselves in the best position to be able to deal with these challenges?

When I was a young man, I wanted to change the world. I found it was difficult to change the world, so I tried to change my nation.

When I found I couldn't change the nation, I began to focus on my town.

I couldn't change the town, and as an older man, I tried to change my family.

Now, as an old man, I realize the only thing I can change is myself, and suddenly I realize that if long ago I had changed myself, I could have made an impact on my family.

My family and I could have made an impact on our town. Their impact could have changed the nation, and I could indeed have changed the world.

—Unknown monk, AD 1100

Be it personal or professional, life is much easier to navigate when we prepare for it, and we *do have* the ability to prepare for it. It means taking care of the basics and leading ourselves first. This is very simple—but not easy. It takes discipline, intent, and thoughtfulness to successfully deploy. Now, you're probably thinking: *C'mon... we all know that! Is this all you got?* But we keep hearing about these important steps—and then simultaneously and blissfully discount them. You don't believe me? Look around you. Our world is full of overworked, stressed-out, unfit leaders whose health is at a tipping point. Their quality of life is in shambles, and they are heading for disaster. When I started writing, I considered pushing this "Leading Self" section to the back of the book...effectively replicating what we tend to do in our daily lives, which is postpone personal wellness to a later time slot. So, at the risk of boring you, I decided to keep this at the forefront of my leadership message because you cannot effectively operate as a leader, a partner, a spouse, or a dedicated parent unless you are healthy and fit. You may have to hear these simple truths one more time. And if this particular time turns out to be your call to action, I will have successfully kick-started your journey to making you a better leader.

I've learned the hard way the price of not taking care of myself first. It happens very easily when you work at a place that never closes, employs thousands, and hosts millions—like the Magic Kingdom. These hard-knock lessons refocused me on the basics.

Chapter 1

Physical Well-Being

*O*n one bleak December morning came the verdict: 226 pounds!
I had "stumbled upon" our scale, which was suspiciously
right in my path from the shower to the walk-in closet. Had my
wife left it there? Was this a coincidence or a deliberate and not-so-subtle
"hint" from my better half? We'll never know, but at that moment, the
number flashing before my eyes had all my attention. This was a first for
me, the "high-water mark" weight indicator that had resulted from many
a day of careless eating, skipping exercise, and generally not giving much
thought to my sense of well-being. It insidiously crept up on me, and it
had not really "registered" until that very morning.

That moment led me to an assessment of my weight, my strength,
my stamina, my sleep, my diet, and, more generally, how physically
comfortable I felt in my own skin. The mental picture I painted was far

from ideal. Guilt set in. Not so much because of the number flashing on the scale, but more importantly because I knew better than to ignore this part of my life. Yet I had not seen it coming. My neglect over time had triggered a slow decline in stamina, a gradual deterioration of my strength, an atrophy of my willpower to exercise.

Some people experience a traumatic event or illness that may result in a sudden drop in their physical well-being, but the vast majority of us are just time's easy prey. We pretend to be victims of a natural process called aging, but we are actually complicit sitting ducks and surrender without much of a fight. Most of us gain a pound or two each year on average, which is negligible enough to overlook, but multiply that by 15, 20, or 30 years ... and you find yourself standing on a scale one morning and wondering, "What happened?" This turned out to be my moment, *my* awakening.

Time to draw a line in the sand and address the problem. There are no specific reasons as to what may trigger your own personal awakening, but because deterioration happens gradually and sneaks up on us, we should all stay vigilant.

The truth is, it doesn't matter if you are 300 lbs or 150 lbs. The most important questions to ask are: "Am I comfortable? Do I feel healthy? Can I perform confidently and effectively? Am I giving myself the best odds to be successful?" There are no norms to conform with, no perfect scenario, no ideal shape or form—just, "Am I physically able to perform at my best?" If the answer is no, it is time to look for solutions.

Unless you live under a rock, you've heard how exercise gives you stamina, the right diet gives you energy, and sleep replenishes the body and soul. So, I am not going to expound on the specific science behind why exercise, nutrition, and sleep are essential, but I will share what worked for me and has helped some of the people I have mentored or coached.

There is just one objective here: lead yourself to a better you. Your path to improving your physical health will be different than mine, and from others' paths. But having a game plan is essential if you want to become the best version of yourself and build the stamina, resiliency, and confidence to lead your family, team, and organization.

Find the motivation.

Fitness has come a long way since ancient times, when the value proposition for keeping in shape was simple: if we were not fit or fast enough, we would either starve to death or something would eat us. Finding enough motivation was easy. Today, we might not literally starve or be eaten if we are not physically fit, but the fitter we are, the more energy, mental clarity, and confidence we have at our disposal.

In my case, running the Magic Kingdom required a great deal of stamina to maneuver around the guests and dodge hundreds of strollers and mobility scooters in the process. Meanwhile, I needed some level of brain functionality to engage with the cast members, make decisions, and serve the guests well. While most office jobs don't require the same level of physical fitness as running a 365-days-a-year theme park, the best leaders do not stay behind their desks all day. They walk around their operation and engage with their colleagues, team members, or clients. They ask questions, probe, investigate, and strategize—and have to make smart decisions in the process. Of course, physical fitness impacts more than our professional life. What about that new hobby we have been meaning to tackle? How about spending more time with our kids goofing around or sharing outdoor activities? What about the volunteering hours we intended to complete?

Once I adopted a healthier lifestyle, my newfound energy and rested body and soul allowed me to achieve much more: I became a would-be kite surfer (still very much a work in progress), I tackled the decluttering project my wife had been pestering me about, and I also picked up some regular house chores, much to her delight. I shared impromptu ultimate Frisbee outings with my kids and volunteered more hours for Junior

Achievement, an organization I have been involved with for more than a decade. All in all, I regained a sense of fulfillment that had been eluding me for some years. Furthermore, my stress and guilt levels dropped. I discovered I could think clearly and objectively about priorities, address issues effectively, and generally be more proactive instead of resorting to my typical knee-jerk reactions.

Your list will obviously be different than mine, but if you are looking for motivation, consider all the things you "mean to do" and "never get to," all the times you say "no" to impromptu invites because you don't have the stamina, and all the quality time you miss because you are too exhausted to do anything else but sleep or collapse mindlessly in front of the TV. What if you could do more with a better version of yourself?

Create a starting point.

Objectively assessing your general well-being on a regular basis is a good starting point. Having a yearly physical is another one. As the saying goes, "What we measure we can improve." Some of us (mostly men) are more reluctant to get an annual checkup—is it our inner macho tendency that prevents us from admitting we're not invincible? Men often cling to the belief that they need to be strong and self-reliant, and statistically do not seek medical advice until they reach their fifties. Whatever your gender, schedule your annual checkup. Do not wait for symptoms to occur or pain to become acute before you see a doctor.

It's important to establish a benchmark of your overall health so that when something goes wrong, your health provider knows just what the "healthy you" looks like. A good relationship with your doctor is equally important, as you'll feel more comfortable being 100 percent honest about everything from your family history, your daily habits (is that *really* just one glass of wine?), and your concerns. Be proactive with the office staff about updating and streamlining records—almost every practice now has patient test results available through a private online portal, which can also connect to referrals and other critical medical information. We've never had so much access to our own health information, so why not take advantage of the resources?

Fit fitness into your busy life.

To find what's right for you, forget about specifics of exercise for a minute. Focus instead on time and convenience; bringing consistency is what really matters. Be realistic. Start by doing whatever works with your schedule. If you've fallen completely out of a fitness routine, now's a great time to experiment. Try setting the alarm clock an hour earlier for a run before work, meet a friend for tennis at lunch, or hit a spinning studio on the way home from the office. Do you like to work out alone? With music? In a class? What gives you an endorphin kick? From cycling and walking to yoga or boxing, options are everywhere. So, no excuses.

Once you find something that appeals to you and works with your lifestyle, block out time on your calendar, and defend that time like you would defend an important meeting. I schedule my workouts just like I would any other meeting. They are *my* meetings with *my body*. If you wait for the skies to open to hit the gym, there will always be more pressing matters, and it just won't happen.

Consider this: We would not let our home deteriorate with mold, broken windows, leaks, and bug infestations. Why? Because its value would depreciate. Likewise, you don't want to let your body slowly fall into decay. It's hard to imagine when you are in your twenties or thirties. Yet it is only a matter of time before aging or self-induced wear and tear takes its toll. You will be able to do less with your body, it will break down faster, and your quality of life and stamina will deteriorate.

Our bodies are ours to keep for life. When we invest in their maintenance by exercising, eating healthy food, and resting, we receive an immediate return on investment in the form of strength, stamina, and power. We also receive a long-term return on investment in the form of longer lives, more and better experiences, and greater success in life and business. So take a hard look at your schedule, carve out the appropriate amount of time to dedicate to your well-being, and stick to it.

Create the best fitness routine.

In February 2019, I turned 50. My high school friends and I planned a celebration trip to an all-inclusive resort in Costa Rica. Needless to say, the late nights were a lot of fun, fueled by exotic cocktails and many stories from our youth that we recount time and time again.

The mornings … those were a little rougher for most of us. No matter. Our friend Missy was determined to get up early and complete what she called "her word" each day. We were all puzzled as to what she meant. "Her word," she explained, was part of an Alphabet Workout routine she followed. Apparently, the Alphabet Workout involved using a list of twenty-six aerobic and strength exercises, such as jumping jacks, crunches, squats, and pushups. Missy had a list from A to Z, with a particular exercise and number of reps next to each letter.

Missy had to complete one "word" worth of exercises per day. For example, if her daily word was *papaya*, she had to do a set of thirty arm curls (fifteen curls per P in *papaya*), 150 jumping jacks (fifty jumping jacks per A), and ten crunches (for the Y). Each day, she had a different word and therefore a different set of exercises to perform. We were all impressed by her willpower, although we learned she had another motivation. Missy was partnering with her 20-year-old daughter, Kaylee. The two of them shared and compared their workouts via their Apple watches. Their individual exercises were different from each other, but they were keeping each other committed. Neither of them procrastinated for fear of being called a slacker. Missy had built a fun and motivating new habit for herself and her daughter, and a "new normal" for her daily routine.

"Start where you are. Use what you have. Do what you can." —Arthur Ashe

Find something fun.

Missy's Alphabet Workout may not be for everyone, but it was fun for her, and she could do it anywhere, anytime, even after a night out that caused the rest of us to sleep in. As simple as it sounds, the best way to fit fitness into your busy life is to start doing something you consider fun and entertaining. If it's fun, we're much more likely to do it when it's cold out, or we're tired, or we find one of the many other creative excuses.

You know yourself better than anyone else, so don't let other people define fun for you, just like you shouldn't let other people define success for you. I prefer to mix up my workouts by alternating among various activities—running, swimming, biking, weight training, skiing, kite surfing, hiking, and the occasional touch rugby game. Find a few activities that you enjoy, and get started. As long as you're moving regularly (and more than you're used to), you're on the right path.

It's about improving.

The only person you should compete against is yourself, so avoid letting other people's fitness influence you. If you are on social media, you'll read stories and see pictures of people who are fitter than you or finishing more extreme workouts. This can be quite discouraging. You will come across well-meaning people who are full of advice, who will tell you all about their workouts and suggest exercise programs and local classes or gyms. We are tempted to emulate them, but keep in mind that they might be months or years ahead of you, that their bodies are different, and their capacity to recover varies from yours. They might have fun doing different things. Learn what you can from them, but stick to *your* plan, *your* idea of fun, *your* own accomplishment. Otherwise, you could end up giving up or even injuring yourself. Remember to run your own race.

Not letting other people's workouts negatively impact our own fitness journeys is tough when you're as competitive as I am. Over time, I've learned to remind myself that physical fitness is not about *winning* but about *improving*. So, when someone shares a fitness success, I congratulate and encourage them, but I have learned not to compare it to my own achievements. Meanwhile, I encourage myself with one idea in mind: if I continue to exercise, I will continue to improve. So, I keep track of my progress and push myself just a little further every day.

I also like to remind myself about the Navy Seals rule of thumb about physical capacity: when you start being mentally ready to quit, you have used up only 40% of your capacity. Logically, that means we *never have* to compete against other people; *we only have to compete against our natural instinct to quit.* If we train ourselves to push until we think we're ready to quit and then keep going, we keep pushing the limit. As our fitness levels improve, our minds will still tell us to quit at 40% capacity—but that level will keep moving, too. We are all just playing a mind game. As Sir Hillary famously said: "It is not the mountains we conquer; it is ourselves." The only way we know what we are capable of is to conquer ourselves. Wouldn't you want to know what you are capable of?

Start small.

When you are just getting started, start small. Push yourself in increments. You don't have to run an Ironman tomorrow—or ever—to be physically fit. You might never run a 5K, but you could be in tremendous physical shape, so don't let marathon runners make you feel like you are not doing enough. Start by going for a walk or bike ride. Walk up and down the stairs for 20 minutes. Whatever the routine, start small, and build in increments. Six months from now, you will be in much better shape if you start small than if you try to go big right away, which often leads to burnout or injury.

Track your progress.

It can be hard to recognize just how far we have gotten with our fitness. This is especially true when we have trained ourselves to constantly push past the 40% mark. When we do that, every workout will feel challenging. So, even though we might be running faster or farther, or lifting heavier weights, we always feel tired. That can make us feel like we're not improving.

To avoid feeling discouraged, I keep track of my workouts. I log the number of days I exercise, number of laps in the pool, sets completed, or miles covered. I gauge my progress by looking at the general trend over time. All kinds of electronic gadgets will do this for those who don't like the old-fashioned paper way. As time goes on, you will be able to visualize several months or even years back. You will see spectacular improvement. And your own progress will give you momentum. Besides, you will be less likely to feel guilty if you end up missing a day or two.

Find a support system.

Even with tools, tracking, and mindset shifts, it takes a lot of willpower to keep going with a fitness program. If you struggle to find the willpower, create a support system. Do you have a 20-year-old daughter to spur you along, like Missy does? That could work. But if you don't, find a coach, exercise with a friend or coworker, or make friends with other people in a group fitness class at the local YMCA to keep you committed. Getting to the gym or going on a run is a lot easier when you have made a commitment to someone else that you will show up. And remember, that person is relying on you, too!

Eat like a healthy gourmet.

As far as I am concerned, Ernest Hemingway accurately captured the essence of French culture when he said, "If you are lucky enough to have lived in Paris as a young man, then wherever you go, it stays with you, for Paris is a moveable feast."

I must be especially lucky because I lived in Paris as a young man while opening Disneyland Paris and married an amazing French wife who has converted me to French culture and, in particular, the French way of eating.

At home, we have a few simple rules.

First, meals are important moments of the day. Be it lunch or dinner (and breakfast on the weekend), they are special occasions at our house, inspired by our time in France. We block out time to gather around the table and enjoy each other's company. We catch up with each other, converse, debate, and sometimes disagree—but we make sure to leave all serious matters and unpleasant conversations off the table, which we consider a safe zone. As a result, we take our time to enjoy our food and have lively conversations at the table.

Second, all forms of electronics remain off-limits during meals. If anyone should be unfortunate enough to deploy a cell phone, he or she is promptly met with a glare and a quick "Holster that!" No TV, no phone, nothing that remotely looks like a screen. This is all about having quality time.

Third, we make it a truly enjoyable food experience, too. The beauty of French cuisine lies in its variety (yes, sometimes frog legs are on the menu!). We eat all kinds of different dishes, often fresh, homemade, and simply prepared. We have always encouraged our kids to be adventurous eaters, with the rule to always give it a try. Taking more time to eat, appreciate our food, and socialize also helps us realize when we are full, and slow eating allows for better digestion. As a result, we stop ourselves before gobbling up another pork chop or going for second or third servings.

Finally, we can eat anything as long as it is with moderation. Do you know what is better for your waistline than a sandwich? Half a sandwich! As I learned during my time at Disneyland Paris, most French people serve much smaller portions than Americans and yet take more time to enjoy their meals. Unsurprisingly, serving portions have gotten bigger in the US, mirroring our expanding bellies. Restaurants tend to pile up food as American clientele often equates quantity with value for money. The truth is, diets are often overrated. There's no need to skimp on your favorite foods. All it takes is portion control. Check the size of your servings and maybe consider using a small dessert plate for all courses; why not? A colleague of mine orders his lunch at restaurants and asks the server to box up half of it before he's even served.

Eating like a gourmet is *the* recipe for a successful yet enjoyable diet. It's nothing earth-shattering, but it works for the French and certainly works for my family. We raised three healthy kids—now young adults who not only take the time to enjoy their meals but would also gladly indulge in *foie gras*, oysters, or frog legs … all in moderation, of course!

Discover your inner Sleeping Beauty.

The final piece of the fitness puzzle is possibly both the easiest and hardest piece to put into place: sleep. In 2014, I was invited to participate in the Sodexho Quality Life Worldwide conference as a featured panelist. The moderator was Arianna Huffington, who had just started what she called her "Sleep Revolution." She would later write an insightful book, *The Sleep Revolution: Transforming Your Life, One Night at a Time* (Harmony, 2016) about the importance of sleep and how it impacts our ability to perform.

Sleep is way too often considered a waste of time. I hear people brag about their ability to perform on only four or five hours of sleep, and I feel sorry for them because I know they are not performing to their full capacity. Virtually every piece of reliable data confirms that sleep is critical to better performance. We can be much more fulfilled and can accomplish more in sixteen well-rested hours than twenty sleep-deprived ones, especially over the long term.

As I learned about the importance of sleep from Huffington and other resources, I started evaluating my emotions and performance after well-rested nights compared to sleep-deprived ones. For years, I bought into the "I don't need sleep" lie. I'd burn the candle at both ends and hang my hat on the fact that I was generally performing well at work and home.

But as I reevaluated my sleeping habits, I realized I would get out of bed feeling beat and grumpy. I was constantly feeling sluggish, running on fumes. I would begrudgingly start my caffeine-infused work day and repeatedly find myself depleted at some point in the early afternoon. My only recourse was another shot of espresso, which would carry me through the afternoon but generally kept me bouncing around until long past a reasonable bedtime. And the cycle repeated itself the next day. I was clearly not logging in enough hours of sleep, and I had gotten myself addicted to caffeine in the process.

It was time for a change. Again, there is no magic number that works for everyone, although many studies suggest getting somewhere between seven and nine hours of quality sleep each night is ideal. When I'm mentoring leaders, I suggest experimenting with what works best for them by tracking how much they sleep and how they felt and performed the following day. Some folks can operate just fine—and feel fine without being constantly caffeinated—with only seven hours of sleep. Others require nine. If you are getting fewer than seven hours of quality sleep on a regular basis, however, you probably need to sleep more.

Assess your energy level as you come out of bed. Do you feel well-rested and ready to face the day? Or, do you feel like a toddler who missed his nap? If you feel like a cranky toddler rather than a well-rested, rational adult, adjust your schedule. Before you go to bed, turn off the TV and stash away the electronics. Much like children, we fare better when we adopt a bedtime routine. So, find one that allows you to wind down. When our kids were young, my wife and I used to take turns reading books to them. This became as much a part of our bedtime routine as theirs. It was our way to wind down and find our inner Sleeping Beauty!

Fast Track to Results

For optimal physical fitness, do the following:

- Create a starting point by assessing your current fitness level. Get a physical exam and commit to scheduling one annually.
- Try the Alphabet Workout! Dancockerell.com/alphabetworkout
- Determine what brings you the most fun and satisfaction and what fits into your schedule. Find a support system if you need one.
- Log your progress and assess improvements by looking at the big picture over a long period of time, not just days.
- You don't have to follow a strict diet if you exercise portion control.
- Do not underestimate the rejuvenating power of sleep. If you are exhausted when you wake up in the morning, you need a new sleep routine.

Chapter 2

Mental Fitness

While studying at Boston University, I participated in the Disney College Program in Orlando, where I worked at the front desk of the Contemporary Hotel for three months. Upon graduation from B.U., I decided to try my luck at Disney again. I was hired as a parking attendant at Epcot, which eventually gave me the opportunity to join the Management Training Program. This, in turn, would later lead me to join the opening team of Disneyland Paris.

At Epcot, I spent a formative six months alternately parking cars or driving the tram that moves guests from the parking lot to the front entrance of the park. It was especially tough during the busy, hot, and humid Florida summer months, but I kept my ears and eyes open and tried to learn and absorb as much as possible. Needless to say that when the opportunity to hone my newly acquired skills in France presented itself, I jumped on it.

This is how, in January 1992, I found myself on a flight bound for Paris. Though I had eagerly volunteered, I couldn't help thinking that I was embarking on a rather challenging endeavor: moving to a country I knew little about, starting a new job with a range of responsibilities I had never held before, and having to do it all in a language I barely understood!

Plus, directing traffic and parking cars in an orderly fashion was a rather easy task in the US, where drivers were mostly compliant, but having French drivers follow directions and wait diligently for their turn was an entirely different proposition! I'd have to handle plenty of other cultural differences, too. Yet I was expected to be the entry-level manager in charge of the parking lot of Disneyland Paris. My mind raced. *What was I thinking? What should I brace for? Frustration? Misery? Ridicule?*

Once I was past the initial moments of panic, I decided to set my mind on a different course. One thing I knew for certain was that I always learned the most valuable lessons when facing challenges. So, I decided to look at this as an incredible learning opportunity that would provide many valuable insights, not to mention interesting stories. I was determined to enjoy the highs and lows that were no doubt headed my way.

Disneyland Paris delivered some hard-knock lessons for sure, but also some pleasant discoveries. Finding out that most French people speak a fairly good amount of English was one of them. But I also worried whether I would meet expectations and understand the French approach to professional life. I soon realized that generally Americans "live to work" while French people "work to live." Our sense of priorities turned out to be radically different and I, as a leader, had to reconcile their approach with American expectations.

I had difficult days when I felt powerless and discouraged—even some days when I was simply tempted to pack my gear and head back home. Every time I thought I had things more or less under control, it seemed that another challenge would present itself: French bureaucracy, disgruntled employees threatening to go on strike, menacing union representatives, aggressive drivers, unethical leaders … the list went on and on.

During my five years of working at Disneyland Paris, I experienced many low points because of what looked like insurmountable challenges. But in the process, I acquired a better understanding of my own strengths and limitations. I also recognized and managed my emotions and frustrations more effectively, and as a result, could understand and influence the emotions of others. In other words, I displayed greater self-awareness and keener emotional intelligence. I also gained a better sense of my personal values that kept me grounded and guided my decision-making during the moments of self-doubt.

While reminding myself of how invaluable this professional and cultural opportunity at Disneyland Paris was, I kept a positive mindset and eventually found myself enjoying living and working in France. Through the good and the bad, I learned lifelong lessons from an incredible experience. As it turned out, I found a career, a way of life, a wealth of insights and, of course, my wife, Valerie.

Mindset

We all see our life experiences through the filter of our mindset. When we acknowledge that this very mindset alters our perception, we are better equipped to exercise control over our lives. After all, as Charles Swindoll famously said, "Life is 10% what happens to us and 90% how we react to it."

Picture yourself behind the wheel of your car in the morning rush hour. We dislike idling in traffic because we are powerless and unable to do anything about it. However, we are very much in control of how we let it affect our state of mind. We can brood, whine, or protest and argue that it is a waste of our valuable time. Or we can opt for a different course of action and make good use of this time. Maybe we're listening to educational programs, keeping up with the news, simply relaxing or, better yet, putting on our thinking caps.

When was the last time you sat in solitary silence, anyway? I am willing to bet this does not happen too often. We live in a fast-paced world where the sheer act of thinking deeply has become a luxury. We are bombarded with information more than ever before but seldom take the time to digest any of it. So why not create value in these rare moments of solitude and exercise that big brain of ours? We cannot do anything about traffic, but we can decide for ourselves if this particular experience will have a negative or positive impact on our daily routine. This is within our control.

My wife and I once attended an award dinner ceremony at Disney during which some frontline cast members were recognized for their out-standing performance. This is a highly coveted recognition, and I had several recipients from the Magic Kingdom in attendance. Three of them sat at our table with their spouses. The event took place a mere four weeks after one particularly devastating hurricane. My wife was inquiring about how everyone had fared during such a difficult event. One couple was quick to respond: "We were ever so lucky!" to which Valerie and I assumed they had suffered no damage to their homes. As we inquired some more, they related how they barely escaped their home to seek refuge at a neighbor's house before their roof flew apart and their house collapsed. As it turned out, this particular family had lost their home and most of their valuables. Yet they were focusing on how much worse it could have been and how lucky they were to have escaped injury or even death… the proverbial half-full or half-empty glass of water. What a display of resiliency, fortitude, and optimism!

"Life is 10% what happens to us and 90% how we react to it." —Charles Swindoll

---

Be your own person.

Thanks to social media, we have become accustomed to parading our ever-so-perfect lives and accomplishments for the world to see. It won't take more than 15 minutes on Facebook to feel pangs of jealousy as we witness the amazing life experiences and exotic travels of our acquaintances. We feel pressured to reciprocate and paint an often glorified picture of our own "perfect" lives.

Which brings me to my next point: life is not perfect. In fact, it can be pretty crappy at times. But we keep trying to live up to the unrealistic standards of happiness and fulfillment on social media. This window on the world puts "keeping up with the Joneses" on steroids: *If everyone's life is perfect, my life should be perfect, too. Why can't my life be perfect?* And down the spiraling cycle we go. When we fail to keep up, we have to face our own shortcomings, insecurity, bitterness, anxiety, or even despair. A 2017 *Harvard Business Review* study found that the more we use Facebook, the worse we feel.

Let's admit once and for all that we have set unrealistic standards for ourselves. Life is tough and unfair at times. Denying it only makes challenges a lot harder to overcome. So let's embrace crappiness! Let's admit that our life is not picture perfect, that we are flawed and do not always get it right, that the weather can be pretty nasty, and we are left out in the cold. This is half the battle. If you can admit to vulnerability and adopt a positive mindset, it will lead you to the obvious solution: learn and grow. This can be quite liberating. No more pretense, no more charade. Just admit that there is always room for improvement, and get to work. The effort will be worthwhile and will make positive outcomes even more enjoyable. Remember, the journey to perfection is a never-ending one.

Dr. Carol Dweck, in her excellent book *Mindset*, defines a "growth mindset" as opposed to a "fixed mindset." The former will allow you to find the silver lining in every cloud, the lesson in every failure, and welcome new tests as learning opportunities. The latter will cause you to steer clear of challenges for fear of failure. As a result, a fixed-mindset leader will avoid risk-taking and rely exclusively on innate talents.

Imagine what happens in an organization led by an individual with a fixed mindset. Attempts to admit and correct flaws are quickly dismissed; inflated egos rely on inflated perception of talents; a restricting pecking order and fear of mistakes inhibit risk-taking—it's all a recipe for disaster. On the other hand, an organization led by a growth-mindset individual will benefit from a leader who commits to bettering him- or herself and also in developing people. He or she will invest in training and promote new ideas and innovations. This forward-thinking leader will constantly challenge the status quo and ask questions. He or she will welcome feedback, constructive criticism, and suggestions from everyone. This eventually gets contagious. Not only will the organization flourish, but the entire team will also thrive thanks to a desire for continuous improvement cemented by its leader.

This idea of growth mindset only strengthens the need for becoming a lifelong learner. You cannot have a successful career by relying exclusively on what you have acquired in college or through your work experience. The pace of change has increased so drastically because of technology and globalization that we can only hope to keep up by educating ourselves. As leaders, we should constantly look to acquire new skills, ideas, methodology, or new ways of thinking. Be an avid learner, be curious, challenge yourself to develop new skills, open yourself to new perspectives, read, read, read…

This thirst for knowledge sat at the core of my motivation for writing this book: not only did I hope to share some insights, but I was also eager to tackle a new challenge and learn a new skill. Admittedly, I had no idea how to write a book (I am pretty sure I never wrote more than a 10-page essay in my college years) and though the task seemed daunting, I was committed to keep ploughing along. Six months later, my book materialized, and I learned a ton in the process.

Someone said, "Walk through life as if you have something new to learn…and you will." I am committed to never losing that sense of curiosity and encourage others along the way. As far as I am concerned, it is never too late to change, never too late to learn, never too late to get better.

Failing does not make you a failure.

Create your own luck.

I'm a firm believer in a direct correlation between our state of mind and our ability to create luck for ourselves. Being naturally curious, I am often looking to interact with people and easily engage in casual conversation. I also happen to have the optimistic point of view that if we stick our necks out and are willing to take ourselves out of our comfort zone, something good will happen. These two dispositions have often resulted in chance encounters and opportunities. I try not to hold preconceived ideas and instead give everyone and everything a shot. Great things often stem out of new encounters and initiatives. Even when the prospects are bleak, I am willing to see the situation through because of the silver lining. Even when things do not turn out to be what you hoped, failures are learning opportunities. Think positively and take risks, and you will inevitably create an auspicious environment for luck.

A great scene from *Apollo 13* illustrates this idea. As a team of NASA engineers learns the fate of the mission and the poor odds of bringing the astronauts safely back to Earth, one of them bemoans, "This is going to be the worst disaster NASA has ever experienced."

To that, the program director responds decisively: "I beg to differ. I believe that this will be our finest hour." And indeed it was. Through collaborative creative thinking, the team brought the astronauts safely back to Earth.

When you remain positive in the face of adversity, good things tend to happen. As a leader, you need to stay open to all possibilities. Be curious, reach out to people, ask questions, seek their opinions, see value in their input and perspectives, and think out of the box. Who knows what's awaiting around the corner?

Two years ago, my wife's cousins were looking to relocate temporarily to the US to learn English. We immediately offered to host them and proceeded to cohabitate for almost a year in what turned out to be a fun and lively experience. They both attended English classes, where they made many friends. We subsequently agreed to host a dinner party for a dozen of their Latin American classmates, who were also in the US to attend a six-month intensive English as a second language (ESL) course. Valerie and I are both keen to meet people from different cultures, and through broken English and much butchered Spanish on my part, we managed to socialize with the group and have a grand old time at our house. By chance, I initiated a lively conversation with one of our guests, Luis.

Luis is a Brazilian entrepreneur. His life story, energetic personality, and enthusiasm piqued my curiosity that evening, and we managed to strike up a great conversation, albeit through many funny misunderstandings. Little did I know that two years later, after I had left Disney and started my new consulting venture, Luis would reach out to me and set me up for some of my first consulting gigs in Brazil with two fellow local entrepreneurs, Felipe and Guto. In turn, these connections have led to multiple engagements in South America.

Had I not volunteered to host Valerie's cousins and their group of classmates, engaged with Luis and shown interest in his personality and career, and agreed to talk to Felipe and Guto, none of this would have taken place. Sometimes, you just don't know where the lucky break is going to come from and who will step up for you. Challenges, mundane situations, and casual encounters may later prove to be a much-needed spark for your endeavors.

Emotional Intelligence

When emotional intelligence or emotional quotient (EQ) landed on our collective radar screens, I was busy opening Disneyland Paris as the

Parking manager. I was too occupied in the details of operational needs to wonder about my EQ or lack thereof. One winter morning, my short-comings hit me right in the face. The locks of the Main Toll Plaza were frozen shut, and we were unable to open them. Soon the guests would be showing up, and we would not be able to let them in. I frantically called Maintenance, and I got a rather lethargic response.

As was often the case with my previous work orders, I heard the inauspicious, "We have a long backlog of requests, but we will get to you." There was no saying as to when the issue would be addressed. Clearly, Maintenance did not seem to consider this a priority, no matter the impact on our operation. I could suddenly sense myself losing it. Out of frustration, I used some colorful language to bring about some kind of urgency to the matter. Before I knew it, I heard myself saying, "You don't get it!"—to which came the stinging and sarcastic response: "Well, you *are* the American expert, after all! Haven't you dealt with ice before?!" What I really wanted to say was, "No, genius! I came from Walt Disney World 'Florid'uh!'" However, I knew better than to go down that path and suddenly realized what I had been doing wrong all along.

There I was in my "all-American glory," bossing around these sea-soned Maintenance workers. I was assuming that my previous six-month tenure at Walt Disney World had sufficiently equipped me to lead a team with diverse backgrounds, skills, and nationalities through the pitfalls of a huge operational opening. Not to mention the fact the French generally looked down on this entire all-American project as a cultural Chernobyl! At no point in time did I look at the "big picture." It did not occur to me to step into their shoes and consider their perspective: a 24-year-old American who can barely string five words of French together becomes their leader, orders them around, puts in requests, and demands their immediate attention—oblivious of their workload and own challenges. It did not seem to them that I had "paid my dues."

My lack of experience had led me to fall back on an outdated transactional and somewhat autocratic leadership style. I had low self-awareness and little control over my emotions. I had been oblivious to the emotional well-being of others, including peers, collaborators, and direct reports. I had failed to forge a relationship with those who were essential to my ability to perform ... and I had just learned that this came with a price.

A Different Approach

Knowing Our Strengths

It is often said that young professionals bring digital intelligence or digital quotient (DQ) to the workplace. On the other hand, more seasoned and experienced workers bring EQ because they can identify patterns of behavior and leverage lessons learned in past situations. They also have a better understanding of their own strengths and weaknesses. This is where we should start. All kinds of assessments are available to help us develop greater self-awareness and determine what kind of personal toolbox we have at our disposal. I have used StrengthsFinder 2.0 and the Myers-Briggs assessments to help me become more self-aware. The results were not necessarily surprising to me, but they helped me consciously direct more energy toward my strengths and passions.

Gallup's StrengthFinders looks at thirty-four different areas and provides an assessment report on top strengths and opportunities. These thirty-four strengths fall into four main categories: executing strengths, influencing strengths, relationship-building strengths, and strategic thinking strengths. I discovered my top five strengths are arranger, responsibility (executing strengths), developer, includer, and responsibility (relationship-building strengths). My Myers-Briggs assessment categorizes me as an ENFP, very much a relationship-based profile.

All this information helped me boil down my priorities to one main realization: *the more time I spent with people, the more successful I was.*

With that knowledge, I adopted a different approach for the rest of my career. Every day, my goal was to be with people and forge relationships, which allowed me to inspire, learn, engage, be creative, gather energy, create excitement, and provide empathy, among many other benefits.

So, what are your strengths? Are you putting yourself in situations where you get to showcase and use them? Ducks swim and squirrels climb. If you are a duck, hang out in ponds; if you are a squirrel, hang out around trees. Place yourself in environments where you can be at your best and use your innate talents to succeed.

To improve self-awareness, nothing is more effective than candid conversations with people you trust and who will provide you with honest feedback. You probably know intuitively who will be the most candid: a friend, a peer, a mentor, a relative, or a spouse. Make a point of consulting someone periodically. Let the setting be casual and relaxed; bring patience and an open mind. As a rule, my wife always mentions her own New Year's Resolution on January 1, and then, for good measure, she will have some "suggestions" for my betterment. It is all in jest, but I always assume there is an underlying reason for her suggestions! Generally speaking, listen intently when receiving feedback or "suggestions," solicited or not. Let it sink in for a while before jumping to conclusions and forging a response or action plan. And always thank your "sounding board" for their input.

When asking for feedback, we too often look for an accomplice.

If you're into writing, start a journal. (I, for one, am a huge fan of bullet journals.) When facing a decision-making point, enter the pros and cons, how you eventually come to your decision, and how you feel throughout the process. Whenever possible, review past comments you have logged. You can see how emotions flow. Patterns will emerge, and you will have a keener understanding of how you react to events and be able to make better decisions. Many self-help groups swear by this therapeutic practice. I've also read that it is a habit of Warren Buffett to log his assumptions and "gut feelings" when purchasing or investing in a company. Later on, he reviews his notes to evaluate if his assessments and instincts were correct. So, there is value in looking into past events, identifying trends, and analyzing our actions. Who am I to argue with the Sage of Omaha, anyway?

Self-Control

Self-control is vital to demonstrating a steady disposition and keeping your feet on the ground. If your goal is to create a great work environmnent for your organization, your team does not want to be dealing with a temperamental and unpredictable leader. At one time or another, most of us have experienced reporting to a leader with a volatile personality—the kind of person who makes you wonder, "What mood is he/she in today?" You don't want to be *that* leader. I have had my "Wreck-it-Ralph" moments, letting my feelings cloud my thinking and making poor decisions in the spur of the moment. So, I have learned the hard way to moderate my reactions. One of my direct reports—let's call him Jeff—was a pretty sarcastic person and would make caustic comments during meetings. I'd let the cynical comments slide to address more pressing matters. Eventually, I convinced myself that Jeff's sarcasm was not that big a deal after all and that most people would find it funny.

It wasn't until a few months later that another leader brought this back to my attention: "Dan, don't you notice what Jeff says? Do you think that it is okay?" Suddenly I became frustrated with myself for not addressing the issue sooner, and letting Jeff's sarcasm become an acceptable behavior. I called him into my office and launched into a very aggressive and emotional tirade about his behavior. Jeff looked at me, startled, as if I were crazy. In his mind, my rant probably came out of nowhere. One day, he was hiking on top of a grass-covered volcano and enjoying the scenery, and the next, the volcano erupted. Had there been the slightest rumble in the air, he would surely have chosen a different route. However, with no warning, he had no reason to change his path.

To take this analogy further, imagine *yourself* as a volcano, emotions roiling beneath the surface. Instead of going into "quiet mode" or "erupting mode," we can learn to have more than two settings: how about a little bit of "rumbling mode?" It's a fair way to give team members a fighting chance to change their behaviors. Granted, this is easier said than done. When you feel like erupting, take a walk, take a few breaths, and strategize your approach—for the next day. Night brings good counsel, and you'll benefit from taking the time to think it over calmly and rationally. If you do happen to spontaneously erupt, then learn how to recover and minimize the damage. It's okay to say, "I'm sorry."

While I've learned to moderate my reactions, I've also discovered delaying reaction can also cause misinterpretation and turmoil. For instance, I personally tend to retreat in silence to ponder an appropriate response. But others can interpret this as a form of passive aggressive "silent treatment." Though not deliberate, my delay in answering or offering a comment on an issue can be perceived as a lack of interest or, worse yet, avoiding making a decision. (On several occasions, my wife or team members have been straightforward in their feedback.) Silence often leaves the door open to interpretation. So if you withhold comment, let it be known for the sake of clarity. You will save yourself from much misunderstanding. A simple "Let me think about it" or "I will get back to you on this" will suffice.

We can improve self-control by practicing mindfulness—the ability to focus on the present and acknowledge a variety of feelings, sensations, and thoughts. It's quite a challenging gymnastic of the mind. But just as we work out to stay fit, we should exercise our brain as well. Regular meditation teaches us to acknowledge our thoughts without being overwhelmed by them. Much like we remove clutter when prepping a house before a showing for prospective buyers, we must remove the clutter in our brain so we can focus on our feelings and better understand how we react. The practice is demanding, and I often find myself lacking the discipline to stay engaged and not let my mind wander. This, too, takes training. Apps such as Calm and Headspace are available to make the practice easier and more readily accessible.

Empathy

After my initial French fiasco in dealing with the Disneyland Paris Maintenance crew members, I took the time to get to know them better. I inquired about their work and frustrations. I asked questions and listened intently. When interacting, I gave my undivided attention: no phone, no side glances. When distracted, I immediately redirected my attention to the conversation. And when faced with challenging situations, I withheld judgment and made sure I understood all the facts and perspectives before articulating an opinion.

As a result, I managed to forge a relationship based on mutual respect for everyone's contributions. I also became aware of the cultural work differences. I made a point of prefacing my requests with the necessary questions about themselves, families, or hobbies, as the local culture dictated. I asked about their likes and dislikes, passions and interests; and shared my own. I even scored some brownie points by leveraging my passion for rugby, which is almighty on French soil! Being more open about myself, my fears, and my worries indicated that I was willing to show vulnerability and made me more approachable. Soon, work requests were fulfilled promptly, and work was getting done. Life had suddenly gotten much easier.

I need to point out a final thought about emotional intelligence and a word of warning: displaying empathy does not mean you have to be nice all the time or agree with anyone or anything. It just means you have the ability to see others' points of view and account for their feelings and perspectives. Let them know that they have been heard and that their opinion matters to you. Then you may choose to disagree ... and that is okay, too.

"Emotional intelligence is not the triumph of heart over head; it is the intersection of both." —David Caruso

---

Communication

More often than not, our lack of self-control can simply materialize in the form of a curt answer, an exasperated remark, a sigh, a side glance, a roll of the eyes, or an impatient twitch. So be aware of verbal and nonverbal cues. When in doubt, I remind myself to take the following steps before a conversation:

- Ask myself if this is the right time and the right place.
- Pay attention to my choice of words and body language.
- Listen avidly and intentionally.
- Look for communication cues, especially nonverbal clues.
- Hold my horses and avoid jumping to sudden conclusions.
- Do not listen with the intent to answer but rather to understand.
- Give myself the gift of time in responding to emotional statements.
- Do not let my perception get skewed by my feelings. Assumptions can easily get in the way.
- Finally, if the conversation gets heated, I ask myself before responding, "Does this really need to be said?"

All these steps are critical during challenging conversations but are much easier to practice in more casual settings. They are important skills to build for any circumstances.

Mindfulness and emotional intelligence will allow you to better understand how you react to different situations and identify your blind spots. Your weaknesses and their trigger points will become more apparent. As a result, you can fight your impulses to react emotionally to challenges, conflict, feedback, or criticism.

The cumulative effects of these simple acts of discipline and self-control will greatly enhance your ability to forge better relationships, understanding, and trust. The Dalai Lama aptly defines this as being able to demonstrate "emotional hygiene."

Leaders who master the art of harnessing the power of emotions—be it theirs or others—are more successful at communicating and inspiring people. They can engage their teams on an emotional level, get their buy-in, and feel more confident about empowering them. As a result, they will be able to drive change more effectively. Because of their keen sense of self and others, they recognize their team members' need for guidance, recognition, and feedback—or simply when it is time to get out of the way.

Fast Track to Results

To achieve mental fitness:

- Adopt a growth mindset and embrace opportunities to learn. You will create your own luck in the process.
- Do not get pressured into unrealistic standards. Embrace imperfection. Be your own person—everyone else is already taken.
- Use StrengthsFinder, Myers-Briggs, or other tools to identify your strengths.
- Create a sounding board of people who will give you honest and open feedback about yourself.
- Practice self-control. If you're frustrated, let the volcano rumble a little before erupting.
- Beware of what may be perceived as passive-aggressive behavior. Let your team or partners know when you need to "think it through."
- Meditate—maybe through the Calm or Headspace apps—to improve your mindfulness.

- Be empathetic: Ask questions beyond the matter at hand, assess the other's point of view, and account for their feelings and perspectives.
- Good communication begins with awareness of verbal and nonverbal cues.

Chapter 3

Moral Fitness

One of the most influential individuals in my life was unequivocally my grandfather Rear Admiral Charles Norville Payne. He taught me the values of integrity, hard work, and humility. As I mentioned earlier, his mantra was, "Do your best, and then forgive yourself." In other words, do what you say you will do, put your best effort into your work, always assume it can be improved upon, and get ready to try again tomorrow. My grandfather lived by his word and led a remarkable life. As a young man, I could only hope to emulate him. I was soon to realize it is not so simple.

Find your moral compass.

Throughout our lives, we acquire a personal set of morals or values. They provide us with a compass to help us make decisions, good or bad, and set the direction for our behaviors. Values do not form organically; they are modeled and influenced by the people who surround us, be it our parents, other relatives, friends, educators, coaches, or spiritual leaders. As we watch these role models, we start to develop an understanding of what is right or wrong, who we want to be, and how we want to lead our lives. Our moral compass determines what we will prioritize and, eventually, with whom we want to associate personally, professionally, and romantically.

As a young man, I thought about my grandparents, parents, sports coaches, and other people I admired. I knew intrinsically that they had the qualities I wanted to emulate in order to become a happy individual. I discovered what I wanted to be known for by watching them in action. They collectively demonstrated respect, humility, hard work, and integrity. They were lifelong learners and great mentors. I never thought of it as acquiring a moral compass per se, but that is indeed what was taking place. It took me quite a measure of introspection until I realized that these qualities were some of the values that I should adopt if I wanted to live a fulfilled life.

So, unbeknownst to me, I had set myself on a personal journey to achieve my ideal self—a journey I'm still traveling today. It begins with being healthy, organized, and reliable. Next is to always be respectful, regardless of the people with whom I interact, and to demonstrate humility and integrity. Last but not least is to be a mentor and leader who helps others reach their potential. I never felt the need to think purposely about my values because I was fortunate to have great role models who steered me in the right direction. Most of this happened subtly.

Some people never consider and wonder about their value system. So, let's try it out. Imagine for a second you were to peruse a long and exhaustive list of values—which ones would you *believe* represent you? You may end up with a long list (we often have inflated opinions of ourselves). But how can you tell whether this list is accurate? Well, there is only one way to find out what you really stand for ...

Align behaviors to values.

Having a list of values is one thing; the real test is to bring personal values to life through everyday behaviors. Having a plan or a wish list is only half the job and clearly the easiest part of the task.

I live in Orlando, where 75,000 people work for Walt Disney World, and I've learned that a good number of them know who I am. On one particular day, I picked up a takeout order at a local eatery and found out that it was incomplete, a recurring issue. I was quite irritated and in a bit of a hurry. The staff looked entirely overwhelmed and poorly trained at best. However, working in the service industry, I knew full well that no one is immune to mistakes, and that most of what I had to endure was probably the result of poor leadership or low staffing. So, I graciously and respectfully asked for the missing items. An elderly employee helped me out, apologizing profusely. When she recognized me, she told me how happy she was to see that Disney executives were also living the Disney values of Respect and Courtesy outside of the Happiest Place on Earth.

As it turned out, her son worked as an entry-level leader on my team at the Magic Kingdom. Imagine what would have happened had I been an absolute jerk about my incomplete order. The family would surely have talked about the hypocrisy of the Disney leaders who required certain standards from their team but not from themselves. On that day, I demonstrated that I walked the talk. I stayed true to the commitment I had made to be respectful with people regardless of their position in life or the circumstances of our encounter.

Having a list of values is one thing; the real challenge is to bring personal values to life through everyday behaviors.

There were a few other instances when I failed to deliver. One particular example occurred when I was leading the Test Track team at Epcot, where I often advocated for teamwork, initiative, and empowerment. For several months, the cast members had been grappling with the fact that seat belts were creating confusion and delay during the guest boarding process. They had tried unsuccessfully to have the issue corrected and were growing frustrated. So, what did I do? Paid attention to their feedback and suggestions; facilitated their attempt at correcting the issue; provided the necessary resources; and thanked them for being proactive? Of course not. After having ignored their plea long enough, I donned my superhero cape, swept in, and singlehandedly corrected the issue by leveraging my almighty manager superpower—which was in retrospect quite easy and admittedly gratifying. I just had to be the hero! Wasn't this what leaders were supposed to do? Where was my promise to empower and reward initiative? As it turned out, the team was disappointed and frustrated, and they let it be known.

Leading a team does not mean you have to do it all. Much like a coach, great leaders should select the various talents for each position; train individuals; set a strategy, expectations, and goals. Subsequently, they move out of the way and let the team execute the plan. But too often, we, as leaders, succumb to vanity (as I surely did that day) and just want to showcase what we are capable of in order to justify why we are in the leader position. In retrospect, this would, and should, have been a perfect opportunity to show the team I trusted them to address issues. I should have supported them in their efforts and let them reap the well-deserved rewards. But I failed to display humility and neglected my promise to empower and support team members.

So, think about your actions objectively. Are you one of those leaders who gives lip service to the team about balance—and promptly denies vacation requests or assigns unrealistic deadlines? How about leaders who brag about availability but are seldom seen in their operation? Do you do what you say you do? Do you demonstrate the behaviors that align with your values? Are you walking the talk? If you fail to do so, you lose credibility. Most of today's elected officials clearly illustrate this point: they are unpopular politicians because their actions look nothing like the promises they made on the campaign trail.

Mind the gap.

Social and cultural cues have a huge influence on our behaviors. For example, many media outlets tend to glorify certain materialistic principles that may affect our ability to live up to our values: self-gratification, prosperity, and power, to name just a few. This often causes confusion and a dilemma, because the temptation to meet the norms of mass media is daunting. As a result, we may want to achieve a certain perceived higher status, run the hamster wheel of financial success, and pursue lofty goals of professional achievements. But ask yourself, "Is this what I truly need to be fulfilled and happy?" If the answer is yes, more power to you. But you may find that you are currently working toward a goal that will not provide you with the level of fulfillment you desire—only a distorted vision of what society promotes. Are we to compromise or give up on our values to keep up with the masses? Are we willing to sacrifice what we stand for? Do we sometimes have to decide between our values and expediency? How about financial success and integrity? You don't have to read deep into a newspaper nowadays to find stories of business leaders or individuals who have thrown their integrity to the wind in order to achieve financial results or some kind of inflated recognition.

In most cases, the discrepancies are mild. We simply stray away from our best intents. It can be easily corrected with a bit of introspection and discipline. There is a temporary gap between who we *think* we are and who we *really* are. It's only human. We do not always stay true to our values. Sometimes this is deliberate, but most times it is unintentional. I like to pride myself on having courage, but sometimes I fail to speak up. I like to think of myself as a hardworking person, but I fall prey to bouts of laziness and procrastination and cut corners occasionally. I hope to be great at teaching but can be impatient with mentees. This simply makes the case for assessing our values and behaviors on a regular basis. In fact, it should be a lifelong exercise. Take a good, objective look in the mirror and remember, people are watching you, and your behaviors speak for themselves. If you find you don't walk the talk, then make amends and correct course.

In other cases, individuals can have a completely different set of values. At that point, the discrepancy is not only radical but often irreversible. It can be a case of mistaken identity because the individual simply does not have the values he claims to have. But sooner or later, the truth will come out. Back in 2000, when I was Operations manager at Epcot, we had hired a new Operations manager externally. The person in question—I shall call him David—had successfully passed the interview process. He had provided the kind of answers leading us to believe he was not only qualified for the job but would also be a right fit for our organization. While David underwent his location training, I was asked to cover his area of responsibility. One day as I was walking his operation, one of his direct reports-to-be approached me and shared an incident involving David. Apparently, David had already spent some time in his operation to introduce himself to his team. While doing so, he felt compelled to point to a poster of *The Lion King* in order to "lay the rules of the land." He told his team that as far as he was concerned, he was "on top of the food chain," much like Simba on top of Pride Rock, and they, on the other hand, were at the bottom of the chain and were to become his faithful laborers. The team was stunned. No one at Disney would think this to be appropriate.

Clearly, David had either not seen *The Lion King* or had totally missed the valuable leadership lessons that transpired through its story! Needless to say, he did not last long. David was promptly sent to find his happiness somewhere else. Yet I could not help wondering how he had passed multiple interviews without eliciting concerns. I knew we typically screened for value alignment to make sure candidates were a good fit in our culture. Could it be that he had provided the right answers, not out of a devious scheme to land the job but simply because he was oblivious of his own behavior and the impact it had on people? Maybe, just maybe, David talked the talk but did not walk the walk and never connected the dots.

In a professional environment, we can doom careers with the distance between our values and our behaviors. While values are the number-one driver of our success, we fail to fully research the values of an organization before we join in. We are too distracted by the compensation package and other shiny benefits. As a result, we may find ourselves operating in a world where we feel a constant pull between what our values dictate and what professional requirements demand. This is not a comfortable situation and a sure recipe for failure. Ultimately, we are left with little choice but to find a better environment where we can thrive or, much like David, we are sent packing in short order.

By the way, finding yourself out of alignment with your organization's values does not always mean you are a bad person, just a bad fit. It's simply easier to succeed in an environment that matches your values.

This exercise in self-awareness is worthwhile. Once we have closed the gap between values and behaviors, we find that there is a clear path to follow, and decision-making becomes a lot easier. It brings consistency to our lives, be it personal or professional. We demonstrate integrity because there is no discrepancy between what we say and what we do. As a result, we build better relationships and foster an environment of trust.

Fast Track to Results

For moral fitness:
- Choose the values that represent you.
- For a list of comprehensive values, go to DanCockerell.com/Values.

To more clearly define your values, ask yourself the following questions:

- What do I want to be known for?
- What do I want people to say about me?
- What makes me the happiest and fulfilled?
- Who are the role models I would like to emulate?

To assess if you are living your selected values, identify the behaviors that support these values. Can you objectively say they are part of your daily routine?

When you join a company, advance in your career, set a goal, or serve a cause, it's time for another gut check. Ask yourself:

- Are my values conducive to achieving this goal?
- Are my values in alignment with the values of the organization?
- Will I be willing to compromise my values to serve that cause?
- Which challenge would cause me to compromise these values?

Chapter 4

Organization, Prioritization, and Planning Skills

I've lost count of the number of times my father has said, "If you don't plan the life you want, you will live the life you get." His words have always been in the forefront of my thinking when preparing for the future. For example, I always thought that one day I would want to leverage my Disney experience to share leadership insights and lessons gleaned along the way. With this in mind, for 19 years, I always readily accepted offers to be a guest speaker for the Disney Institute. This department provides outside organizations with training on Disney's approach to quality service, training, and leadership, among other topics. Participants are always eager to meet Disney executives and I, for one, always took the opportunity and used it to hone my speaking skills. When time came to start my new consulting and keynote speaker career, this experience served me well, and I transitioned smoothly to my new role.

Planning is essential, especially considering the pace at which we operate today, which demands that we quickly adapt to change. In order to live our best lives, we must not only plan for the future and organize our time efficiently but also spend that time on the right activities.

First and foremost, we should all remember that we don't have a *personal life* and a *professional life*. We have *one life*, and we should address it holistically. If you disagree with me, I refer you back to what I wrote earlier on physical fitness. If you don't schedule your workouts, chores, and doctor appointments as scrupulously as your professional appointments, you will come to pay the price in the long term. For that reason, it is best to have *one calendar* where you log in all your tasks. Heck, I even include my dog's heartworm medication regimen on my calendar!

Too often, I meet high-performing leaders who have a strategy, priorities, and plans for their areas of responsibility at work using scorecards, resource analysis, and regular check-ins to measure progress. But for some reason, these same leaders fail to apply the same organizational principles to their personal life. This is a step backward because simple organizational skills and time management can dramatically reduce stress both at the office and at home.

Plan for the unpredictable.

Most leaders are, at a minimum, somewhat organized (or just happen to have a terrific assistant who keeps them out of trouble), but few realize that being organized isn't just about getting everything on a to-do list done. It is about having the important, long-term tasks on that list taken care of *and* being available to handle all the other urgent, important things that come up every day.

There are few places where this is more of a necessity than at Disney. I never, ever knew how my day would turn out. I'd tell my family that I'd give them 1,000 guesses about what I had dealt with that day, and that I was 100 percent sure that they would not be able to guess it.

The conversation would often go like this:

"Hello, honey, how was your day?"

"Well ...

- "A helicopter landed in the parking lot for some reason ...
- "Someone brought monkeys dressed as clowns in a stroller into the park ...
- "We found a handgun in a pirate boat ...
- "A big brown bear was hanging out in the campground showers ... and
- "Two Dopeys showed up with the other five dwarves. And we still can't find Doc."

Such is the life of a Disney leader. And while your own kingdom may not contain quite the same scenarios, we are all thrown curve balls. What to do?

Once I realized that there was no possible way to avoid the unpredictable, I started planning for it. Simply put, I kept windows of flexible time in my schedule to address whatever would be thrown at me, be it helicopter landings or multiple Dopeys.

Great leaders are able to improvise and react spontaneously to whatever issues come up. This is why having a plan *and* flexibility is so important. When these issues pull you off track, having that wiggle room to maneuver will snap you back to *your* plan.

So instead of being a victim of these urgent issues, I planned time in my day to react to them and expected them. I did not overschedule myself and did my best to avoid back-to-back meetings. Also, I scheduled time to eat lunch. These breaks gave me more time to react to requests without throwing my whole day off. You can plan for the unexpected!

Do the right things at the right time.

The Eisenhower Matrix is a great tool that helps me bring clarity to my time-management process.

As the Allied Forces Supreme Commander during World War II and the 34th president of the United States, General Eisenhower had to make tough decisions continuously. He famously said, "What is important is seldom urgent, and what is urgent is seldom important." Based on this, he created the following matrix to categorize to-do items according to the most critical parameters of Importance and Urgency.

The Eisenhower Decision Matrix

	Urgent	Not Urgent
Important	**Do** Do it now.	**Decide** Schedule a time to do it.
Not Important	**Delegate** Who can do it for you?	**Delete** Eliminate it.

As the matrix shows, we must minimize the **"Not Important/Not Urgent"** items that bring little to no value: social media, coffee breaks, pointless routines, unproductive meetings, and duplicated efforts, among others. Let's face it: we all have some of these hidden in the nooks and crannies of our agendas. You can earn back a gold mine of valuable time by assessing the impact of trivial activities. It's time for a thorough spring cleaning to get rid of the dead weight. These items have got to go!

The **"Not Important/Urgent"** box includes things that need a response or action—but not necessarily by you! This is your "delegate" box. People around you *want* to take on more responsibilities and are capable of doing so. Take some risks and see where you can delegate tasks you always thought you had to manage. You will be surprised about how many time-consuming activities you can eliminate by allowing others to approve and decide. Letting go is a very hard thing to do. Our ego sometimes gets in the way, or we resist passing on a particular task because we simply enjoy taking care of it. More often than not, we cling to authority out of fear of mistakes or a sense of self-importance. But delegating shows that you trust your team and you are looking to develop them. You will be surprised to see how motivated they are to step up. It is not that hard if you follow these three simple rules:

1. Set clear expectations, and define what needs to be accomplished.
2. Make sure they have the right tools and resources.
3. Keep an eye on things, and monitor from afar. Step in to correct course and provide guidance if needed.

The payoff is immediate! Not only will you instill an environment of trust in your organization, but you will also gain much valuable time for yourself. Consequently, you will be able to spend more time on making a difference in other areas.

It is also wise to remember that although you can delegate your *authority* to others, you can never delegate your *responsibility*. This is a message you should live by and communicate to your team. So, delegate with caution and care on a regular basis.

We cling to authority out of fear of mistakes or a sense of self-importance. But delegating shows that you trust your team, and you are looking to develop them.

The **"Not Important/Urgent"** box also includes factors that have the illusion of importance but are actually imposters. Technology interruptions, repetitive administrative tasks, unnecessary meetings, and other people's problems can all seem important—and they may be to others—but they are not always important to you as a leader.

The "**Important/Urgent**" box is defined as items that need to be addressed immediately and can only be addressed by you. This is just the nature of many jobs. As I mentioned, we cannot predict when these will occur, but we have to plan because we know they will. Think of the firefighters at your local station. They do not know when they will need to respond to the next fire, but they know the bell will ring eventually—and when it does, they need to be ready to roll. Just be prepared by allowing flexibility in your schedule to address impromptu issues.

The **"Important/Not Urgent"** items are also the ones that only *you* can deliver. The difference, though, is that these issues, unlike urgent issues, do not have immediate consequences. This is where you can focus on big decisions, strategize, prepare for big projects, look for improvements to your operation, consider and plan for the future, and generally do your best thinking. The Eisenhower Matrix method advocates scheduling these items for an appropriate time. Keep in mind this will only work if you are sure that your "appropriate" time won't be taken away by some unexpected emergency. Unfortunately, that was often the case when I worked at Disney, so I adopted a slightly different approach based on the old saying, "The only way to eat an elephant is one bite at a time." I consider the items in my "Important/Not Urgent" category my elephants. (My favorite, world-class veterinarian, Dr. Mark Penning, may object to the analogy, but no worries, I have no desire to ever taste an elephant!).

My thinking goes like this: As long as I "eat a bite" of my elephants every day and spend a small amount of time thinking about them, researching them, and making a tiny step of progress, I can slowly gobble them up. At Disney, I sometimes found myself struggling to balance my time between delivering today's results and planning for the future. This, in fact, is one of the major challenges of being a leader. You need to have the discipline to shift your focus back and forth between the two. So, whenever an opportunity presents itself, I work toward making progress on my "elephants." Little steps can make a huge difference. As James Clear writes in *Atomic Habits*, if you get one percent better each day for one year, you'll end up thirty-seven times better at the end of the year.

Be mindful of how it plays out.

With better organization and clarity of goals, I can move many vital items into my "Important/Not Urgent" box. That is always the goal. Unfortunately, the "Important/Urgent" items never seem to entirely go away. I'm sometimes thrust into important activities because of my own lack of planning or foresight. Other times, I receive urgent requests to address immediately. More often than not, it is simply the nature of business.

As I mentioned, I often lived in that box at Disney. When an operational issue caused a Disney cruise ship to delay its return to Port Canaveral, the Walt Disney World operation had to handle 2,000 would-be passengers stuck in Orlando for three days with no room reservations. Lucky me—I was tasked with organizing a mock-up "front desk" at Epcot where we processed the said guests and directed them to available rooms either on Disney property or nearby. Two thousand people is a lot of rooms, and a mountain of bags and suitcases to boot! My team and I quickly took care of the situation. Everyone stepped up, and we were able to complete the task at hand.

This is the kind of scenario that can throw you off track for a day or even a week. The stress from working on these unpredictable events will take a toll on anyone. Hence the need to operate under these three conditions:

1. Being both physically and mentally fit so you don't crumble under pressure. If you faithfully schedule and follow your fitness plan, it will prepare you to cope with particularly stressful situations.

2. Having a planning tool like the Eisenhower Matrix that helps you bring clarity when sorting through the to-do list during challenging times.

3. Being surrounded by a team you can rely on, knowing exactly what they can handle for you. If you have tested the waters by empowering your team members on a regular basis, you will know their capability. You will know whom you can trust to

take over some of the decisions when it is crunch time. Do not wait to be in crisis mode to start delegating.

On any given day, I would refer to my own matrix and address my "Important/Urgent" box first thing in the morning. Did I tell someone that I would call them today? Was there an email or a response that required immediate attention? Did something just arise and need swift decision-making? At the Magic Kingdom, you can bet the answers to these questions were yes, yes, and yes. So, I would get up early, get as many of the important, urgent items done, and then dive into the important, not urgent work, my "elephants." If the plan worked well, the urgent issues arising during the day could either be delegated or I would use some of my scheduled flexible time to get them done. These open slices of time did not always stay open for long. But when they did, I would walk the park or have a quick lunch at the cafeteria with frontline cast members, which allowed me to keep a finger on the pulse of my operation. I uncovered and heard a great amount of valuable information this way. As a result, I could anticipate issues or learn of new suggestions and ideas.

Make it count.

I'd like to share one final insight on the subject of organization. Nowadays, we are bombarded with all kinds of information, options, and demands that we all have to sort through. As a result, we are pulled in a million directions at once. This results in what I call the "squirrel" effect. If you have ever seen a squirrel darting in front of a car, you've noticed how they seem to change course multiple times before committing to a direction. It's a case of what many people now call FOMO (fear of missing out) or FOBO (fear of a better option). We have all been in that situation, not knowing which way to go and changing our minds over and over, or getting distracted from what we are trying to accomplish. This causes many commitment issues in our professional and personal lives, and more generally with how we use our time.

The solution is simple (again, do not confuse simple with easy): take your time to make well-thought-through decisions, and then commit to stay the course and see it through, not letting distractions pull you away from your goal. If you are starting a new initiative, support it 100%. If you are spending time with someone, turn off your phone, and make it quality time. I once walked the Magic Kingdom with Bob Iger, CEO of the Walt Disney Company, and as we made our way through the park, he stayed shoulder to shoulder with me and listened intently when I talked. I was also impressed to see the dedicated attention that he gave the cast members who crossed our path. I am sure there were a million other things that could have distracted him from the task at hand, but he made sure to provide a quality interaction with everyone. It was an impressive example to emulate.

Likewise, if you spend time with someone, be it professional partners, kids, or spouse, make it count. Time is a rare commodity. You will not get back what you have wasted. So stay focused, stay on course, and don't be a squirrel.

Fast Track to Results

For organizational fitness:

- Adopt a holistic approach to organization. Combine your professional and your personal agendas and list of goals.
- Prepare for the unexpected. Allow yourself slices of time to respond to urgent matters.
- Create your own Eisenhower Matrix, using the chart earlier in this chapter. Now, what must you do, decide, delegate, or delete?
- Don't wait for a crisis to strike to start delegating. Make it a usual occurrence and know the capabilities of your team.
- Tackle your "Important/Not Urgent" tasks "one bite at a time."
- Don't get distracted. When it comes to investing time, favor quality over quantity.

Part 2:

Leading Team

Like many American teens, I grew up loving football. I played through most of my youth and starred on my high school team as the highest-scoring running back. I imagined myself playing in college, and eagerly became a walk-on for the Boston University team my freshman year. This turned out to be one of my most stinging lessons in humility: I quickly found out I was not fast enough, strong enough, or nearly good enough to play at the college level. More importantly, I knew it would be a while to get there, if ever.

Through a string of lucky encounters, I instead joined the rugby team and developed a passion for the sport. In case you are not familiar with rugby, I'll explain: it is very similar to football minus the pads. Protective gear consists of mouthguards and taped ears. It is rather rough and often referred to as "a sport of hooligans played by gentlemen." I find this to be a true description as matches, though fierce, intense, and sometimes violent, usually end up with both teams sharing rounds of beer during rugby's notorious "third half."

Other than the camaraderie and athleticism, several aspects of rugby appealed to me. Later on, I recognized these as essential not only to the sport but also to organizational success. First of all, rugby players come in every shape and size. The stocky and strong ones (the forwards) shield, tackle, and will make any necessary contact to win or retain the ball—generally banging heads against each other for most of the match. Real brutes. The faster ones and slender backs use their speed to break through the defensive lines, thus staying out of the fray … most of the time. The diversity of talent is necessary to the team much like in any business team. It takes an assortment of strengths to be successful, and a great leader must have the ability to identify and recognize everyone's talent.

Secondly, I consider rugby the ultimate team sport: the dynamics of the game are such that everyone can move the ball forward, and everyone on the team can score regardless of his role, yet no individual can do it alone. To make matters just a bit more challenging, a player can only make a pass *back* to his teammate, which means that you must always be present in a supportive role and trust that your team will also "have your back" and be there for you when needed. I found that to be a prerequisite for any leadership role throughout my career. Sometimes you carry the ball forward, and sometimes another team member does—and you had better be there to help.

Last but not least, I was lucky to captain several teams at B.U. I realized that I wasn't the strongest, fastest, or best player on the team, but I could rally the troops and make sure we would perform to the best of our ability. Much like a business leader, I had to set an example for everyone to follow, so I was diligent with my fitness and training. Then I had to make sure everyone was as ready as can be on game day. This took a bit of shrewd creativity, but my strategy was well honed: Rugby players are notorious "socialites," so I'd organize a party on Thursday nights and make sure the team had a grand old time. As a result, players would be too exhausted to go out Friday, the eve of our matches. It was a sure way to guarantee they were rested and ready for Saturday games. (As the saying goes, "The end justifies the means."). I also had to pay attention to all the different players on the team: the new ones who were trying to decide if they would continue; the wild ones whom I needed to reel back; the quiet ones who sometimes needed an encouraging word; and the veterans whom I could count on to support me.

Much of the skills I acquired while playing rugby proved to be valuable when I became a leader at Disney. I learned about appreciating the value of different talent, team collaboration, trust, setting an example, and the importance of relationships.

Chapter 5

Selecting and Retaining New Talent

hen I became the Operations manager of Disney's All-Star Resort, I spent about eight weeks in immersive training. My only hotel experience to that point had been working as a front desk host at the Contemporary Resort during my college program. I was now responsible for the Front Desk and the Housekeeping operations of a hotel with 1,920 rooms. As I had done in every other role, and as is the custom at Disney, I received the appropriate costume (in keeping with the assumption that Disney team members are actually being cast in a show, we refer to uniforms as costumes) and started to train in each position of the hotel.

I learned how to check guests in; how to reserve rooms for guest preference and length of stay; and how to book dining reservations. I also learned how to handle firsthand the various requests and complaints from guests.

Then came the humbling and incredibly educational two weeks of my training: Housekeeping! At the All-Star, each housekeeper is assigned eighteen rooms per day to clean. Some are stayovers and some are check-outs. On average, a Disney housekeeper gets seventeen minutes to clean a stayover room and twenty-eight minutes if the guest has checked out. By the end of my two-week training, I managed to clean only fourteen rooms in a shift, no breaks, no lunch. Ever since this experience, I leave a very generous tip for every housekeeper at any hotel I stay in. Having "been there," I can empathize with how hard they work!

What does this have to do with selecting and retaining talent? Well, let me tell you about Blanca, my housekeeping trainer. Blanca did her best to show me the secrets to cleaning rooms fast and still maintaining the Disney cleanliness standards. No matter how quickly I tried to clean, I ended up making several trips out to my supplies cart, had to walk around the bed multiple times to make it, and missed many of the details that Blanca hit.

One day, during the end of my training, Blanca told me that she was going to do a deep inspection of one of my rooms and show me the expected level of detail. I cleaned and dusted and checked everything twice before she came into the room with her white glove.

She made her way through the room, checking my suspect hospital corners on the beds and looking for dust on all the ledges. Eventually, she went into the bathroom and asked me to come in. "Dan, did you clean the bathtub?" she asked. I told her that the bathtub was clean, so why was she asking? She would not back down and asked me again—in the way a mother asks her child if they brushed their teeth. "Dan, did you clean the bathtub?" By this time she had her finger in my face, and I felt like *my* mom was grilling me. Finally, I sheepishly admitted that I had not because it *looked* clean, and I wanted to focus on the rest of the room.

I had two questions for Blanca. The first was the one any kid asks when they get busted. "How did you know that I didn't clean the bathtub?" She told me that, for one thing, the tub was dry: "At least splash some water in the tub if you want it to look like it has been cleaned!" Apparently, not the perfect crime. My second question was, "Blanca, if the tub is clean, then why do I need to clean it?" She took a step back and explained to me. "Dan, the only way to keep a tub clean is to clean it while it looks clean. As soon as the mold or mildew starts to appear, you are too late! These rooms have to be impeccable, and I want the best for *my* guests!" She was a proud perfectionist and took full ownership of *her* rooms and *her* guests. Well there you go, my first glimpse into talent in action: her attitude!

I asked Blanca where she learned that approach to cleaning, and she proudly shared that her mother had taught her. I met many housekeepers who had their own secrets to success in keeping their rooms clean, and I mean *their* rooms. I was surprised by the sense of ownership and pride, and their attitude toward their craft. Unbeknownst to me at the time, some of our return guests often requested a particular room or section of the hotel because of the care and attention they had received from a specific housekeeper during previous visits. They knew the cast members by name and looked forward to being in their care. The feeling was mutual. You would think the housekeepers were hosting family members!

You can impart the right skills, not the right attitude.

Let me tell you one more story about superstar talent. Deb came to my team at the Magic Kingdom as we were transitioning to a new organizational structure. She was told that she needed to get some operational experience in order to move on to the next level at Disney. It had been years since Deb had been leading teams in daily operations. She had a lot to learn about the ins and outs of running Space Mountain, Buzz Light-year's Space Ranger Spin, and Cosmic Ray's, one of the highest-grossing restaurants in the world. I was not concerned with her temporary lack of knowledge and skills, because we had a strong team at the Magic King-dom, and I knew that if she took the time to learn and immerse herself, she would gather the technical skills she needed to lead the group, which she did quickly. She was a high achiever and inspired her team to look for continuous improvement.

Deb's mindset, positive attitude, and energy were what really made her successful. She quickly managed to build a great culture in her depart-ment. Her team stayed positive through thick and thin and proactively dealt with any challenges. A constant low roar seemed to be coming from her office or conference room. It was one of my favorite activities to barge into one of her staff meetings, feign anger, and bellow: "What the heck is going on here? We're trying to get work done next door!"

Deb would say with a smile: "Welcome to the meeting, boss, glad you could join us. Hey, guys, tell Dan about your new idea!"

Her positive, playful approach to work was infectious. She brought in energy every day to share with whoever wanted some. Much like Blanca in Housekeeping, Deb had a drive to be great at what she did, took pride in her work, and, in her case, brought her direct reports and anyone nearby along for the journey.

So, how can we find the Blancas and Debs of the world? How can we identify the right talent for our teams, and then make the most of that talent? How do we make sure the talent we assemble are the right ones for the team and complement each other? How do we see beyond our own preconceived ideas and enlarge the scope of talent for our organization?

Identify the right skills ("Can you do the job?").

Let's start with the word *talent*. What usually comes to mind is skill. I think about business professionals performing at the highest levels. Like athletes, musicians, or artists, they can identify a talent to use productively, and they turn that talent into a skill by developing it. There are limited ways to do this, and it takes time and focus.

Malcolm Gladwell popularized the theory that 10,000 hours is the magic number needed to become great in a chosen activity. Many others have pointed out flaws in this theory. Regardless, one has to be ready to put in a lot of time to practice and have the talent embedded. Now, I am not saying that we cannot become *good* in any endeavor, but the truth is that we can only become *great* in one, maybe two areas. I, for one, cannot sing. No matter how much time and practice I'd put in, I still wouldn't be able to hit a note with a stick. I simply do not have the talent to ever become a great singer. Such is life!

I used to think that I could motivate, train, and encourage anyone to be great at anything. Then, Valerie and I had three kids, and I threw that idea right out the window. I became convinced that our talents are wired into us. How could three children who grew up in the same house, were raised by the same parents, and attended the same school be so different? Any parent who has more than one child understands this very well. Valerie and I concluded early on that we were not going to change our children to fit a mold we wanted. It was clear that we needed to help them identify their talents and then encourage and support them to develop those talents into skills.

There is obviously a difference between having children and hiring employees for our organizations—namely, you don't hire and can't fire your kids! (Although, we certainly researched that option at certain times in our kids' teenage years.) But the same principles translate into the corporate world: People already have certain embedded talents. It is a leader's role to identify these talents and give team members an opportunity to turn them into skills. It took Blanca much practice to perfect her routine to most efficiently clean those rooms. Today, she knows how to organize supplies in her cart, make a bed without going back and forth, and do proactive cleaning. Only through practice and experience did she acquire these skills. We can easily learn some of these from others, but it takes time to reach perfection and make them second nature.

How about skills at the leadership level? As I mentioned earlier, I highly recommend using StrengthsFinder 2.0 as a guide to identifying your talents—specifically the soft skills required from someone in a leadership position. To reiterate, these are broken down into four categories: executing skills, relationship skills, influencing skills, and strategic thinking. Consider which talent you need to bring to your team and which skills are required for your mission. You may not get it right every time as such skills can be subjective, but this methodology will remove some of the pitfalls in your selection process. Listen to the stories people share about their previous experience. How do they work with a team? How do they communicate? How do they provide feedback and recognition? How do they deal with challenges and deadlines? If no details are forthcoming, chances are they do not excel in these skills or simply do not have experience in these areas.

As for the technical skills, I am a firm believer that, much like Deb or I did during our onboarding process, every leader should spend as much time as reasonably possible working in their operation and learning the ropes. There is no way around it if you want long-term success and credibility.

Identify passion ("Do you want to do the job?").

One of the nineteen positions I held at the Disney Company involved a stint in Human Relations. I consider myself to be a people person and willingly stepped in, looking forward to acquiring new skills. I quickly found out that working in HR actually got me further away from what I liked most: interacting with people. At one point, I was assigned a project to improve guest and cast interactions. I could certainly dig into my experience as an operator to drive the project forward, but I was very much an individual contributor in that particular position. I did learn a ton but discovered that I had little taste for this support role. My heart was in Operations, where I could be in the middle of the fray. Clearly, my passion was lacking, and it probably showed in my performance. Fortunately, this was short-lived, and I was relieved when I got reassigned to the park.

Passion may be another subjective element to measure, but it sure makes a huge difference in performance. Both Deb and Blanca love what they do. It shows through their energy, pride, desire to improve, and commitment to their roles. Their level of professionalism and pride are not transferable nor can they be taught. So when you interview a candidate, do you hear excitement, pride, and enthusiasm? All are indicators of future performance. Is this particular candidate interested solely in the compensation package, or will he or she truly be looking forward to the job? You can bet that if the former is true, the commitment to the job will quickly fizzle as it surely did for me in HR. If the latter is true, you'll be hiring someone eager to come to work every day and tap into a reserve of energy, creativity, stamina, and commitment that only passion can trigger.

Identify attitude ("Will you excel at the job?").

As far as I am concerned, this is the single most important condition to great performance: attitude! Will this candidate say "yes" to changes? Will this candidate be willing to get out of his or her comfort zone? Will this candidate be willing to learn? Will this candidate overcome barriers and roadblocks? Will this candidate refuse to take "no" for an answer? As I discussed in the earlier chapter about mindset, having the ability to think positively in the face of uncertainty and find the resources to overcome obstacles is essential to success no matter the position you hold, be it frontline or leadership. The right attitude is the deal breaker. Many success stories were founded on great attitude, and many careers were doomed *because* of poor attitude. In the words of Jack Sparrow in *Pirates of the Caribbean*: "The problem is not the problem; the problem is your attitude about the problem."

Identifying great attitude may sound challenging if you don't know which questions to ask. Carol Quinn, the author of *Motivation Based Interviewing*, has created a very simple and yet effective technique of targeted questions (read more in her book). I find it to be a great tool even if you are not a Human Resources specialist. Not only is it a straightforward way to acquire better interviewing skills, but it is also a great tool to identify skill, passion, and attitude in every interaction.

Build a diverse and inclusive team.

During my tenure as the vice president of the Magic Kingdom, I started to invite Matt, one of the junior industrial engineers, to my weekly staff meeting.

For context, Industrial Engineering has played a pivotal role at Walt Disney World since its opening in 1971. As "Operations Research Analysts," they are high-level problem-solvers who use advanced techniques, such as big data mining, optimization, statistical analysis, and mathematical modeling to come up with solutions that help businesses and organizations operate more efficiently and cost effectively.

Bruce Laval, or as we warmly refer to him, "the father of Industrial Engineering" brought this approach to Disney theme parks and forever changed the way we planned and operated these magical places.

Industrial Engineering's contribution is priceless. In fact, I would never make a big decision without our industrial engineers weighing in.

Back to Matt.

Some of my direct reports at the general-manager level questioned the value of his presence because of his youth and low seniority. My point of view was simple: he is young, unbiased, has a set of skills none of us has, looks at the park operation in a different way, and raises questions that we would not have otherwise considered. What's not to like? I could not see any downside to his presence, and I was proven right on many occasions. Matt suggested several positive changes based on his study of park data, analysis, and his personal experiences working in and observing the park operation. He was humble, smart, and not intimidated to offer his opinion. Best of all, he had a winning attitude toward everything he did.

The merits of bringing diversity to a team are well established, be it a diversity of talent, gender, generation, perspectives, opinions, or backgrounds. It is a no-brainer as far as I am concerned, and one would be foolish to deny the upsides of a professional "melting pot." However, it is also well documented that we generally gravitate toward people who look, think, and behave like we do, if only to stay within our comfort zone. Look around you: Do the people you surround yourself with all look alike? How about gender? Age? Race? Do you all have the same background or career paths? Do you all operate at the same level? Do you all ask the same questions? Chances are the answer is often yes. Why? Because if we are not purposeful about diversity, we will just stay within the safe boundaries of what we know and feel comfortable with.

This was a problem we wrestled with at Disney. We intellectually understood the value of diversity. We would find external candidates and tell them that we wanted their fresh perspective and novel approach, and we wanted them to challenge our thinking. However, once they started working, we took them through the onboarding process and explained how things worked—and when they offered new ideas and opinions, we would quickly try to justify why that would not work at Disney. We wanted new insights but simultaneously beat newcomers into submission until they relented and started to think the "Disney" way.

Building a diverse team is only the starting point. Many companies hire a "token" diversity team member only to try to mold that very person into their way of thinking or worse yet, squish their attempt at bringing a different approach. Diversity serves a purpose only if it is accompanied by inclusiveness. A great leader has to be willing to listen and give others a voice. More importantly, a leader must listen to different ideas and perspectives and stay open to being challenged. Diversity is being invited to the party; inclusiveness is being asked to dance.

One other point I'd like to make about diversity: I consider myself an open-minded person and welcome people of different ages, genders, races, backgrounds, sexual orientations, religions, and opinions with interest and curiosity. However, no matter how self-aware and welcoming we are, we all make assumptions that can be revealed in subtle ways. For example, one time, a female direct report who was new to my team and had transferred over from a support role had returned from maternity leave. I knew her transitioning in both work position *and* as a new mom would be challenging, so I made a point of telling her that I would be supportive and make sure she gets the necessary balance in her life to take care of her newborn.

Before I talked any further, she cut me short, "My husband and I have discussed the matter, and I expect to be kept accountable in my job like everyone else regardless of my 'new mom' status." I was surprised by her response and thought her tone was rather curt and assertive. When I got home, I related the interaction to my wife who immediately asked, "Would you have made the same comment to a new dad?" She brought out the obvious. As much as I was trying to be helpful and supportive, my comment would not have crossed my mind had I been dealing with a male team member. Where my intent was to show empathy, I realized I was making assumptions that were flawed and biased. Clearly, this couple was sharing the load of parenthood responsibilities and were well prepared for their new life as a family. My assuming it would affect my female team member's performance was presumptuous at best.

Create plans for retaining new talent.

More than 7.1 million jobs are unfilled in the US today. We are all competing for the best talent, and since it is a worker's market, people have choices. Additionally, marketing open positions, interviewing, and training has a cost to the company, as does the lower productivity of being short staffed. Isn't it just easier to get great people and have them stay? That is one of the superpowers of a strong culture.

Most workers who leave their organizations quit in the first 90 days. When we are new, it is easy to walk away. We have not yet built relationships with coworkers, and we are under a lot of stress learning the job—figuring out how to navigate the rules of the company, the commute, etc. This is when workers are most vulnerable and likely to leave. It is the most important time for the company to provide extra support, to nurture, and to mentor. Make sure these new workers feel comfortable, and assure them that they made the right choice joining the company. We never get a second chance to make a first impression.

Over the years, I have found an effective tool to be the 30/60/90 day retention plan. For each new hire, assign a manager to keep an eye on the new employee, check in with them weekly, and have a sit-down at the end of their first week, first 30 days, first 60 days, and first 90 days.

Match an employee "buddy" to answer new hires' questions, show them the ropes, provide moral support (you can even put some motivation in place for the mentors, and reward them if their mentee stays past the 90 days).

Additionally, create a consistent questionnaire for each new hire check-in, focused on appropriate issues, respectively, for week one, and then 30 days, 60 days, or 90 days. After week one, you may want to focus on learning about them, their background, experience, and motivation to join the organization. This is also a great opportunity for the leader to tell the new employee about their own background and give any tips that may help in the new job. It is the beginning of forming a relationship, and so should make it more difficult to leave the job!

Sample 30-Day Check-In Questions

- *Have you figured out the timing for your commute?* (This could also include school drop-off for kids and other logistical issues.)
- *So far, is the job what you expected it to be? Are you feeling challenged by the position? Are there any key areas you feel like you are excelling or maybe need more training?*
- *Do you feel you have the information, tools, and resources you need to do your job successfully? Are you feeling welcomed by other unit staff?*
- *Are you experiencing any challenges in particular that I can assist you with?*
- *Are you feeling comfortable within the organization in general? Do you feel like you have a good understanding of your role within the organization?*
- *Do you feel you are able to be productive and effective in your position? Can you discuss why or why not?*
- *If you could go back 30 days, is there anything you would do differently? Anything you think we could do differently?*
- *Do you feel you are receiving enough feedback and assistance from your leaders?*

Sample 60 and 90 Day Check-In Questions

- *What areas/tasks/projects are you enjoying the most within your position? Are there any new skills that you feel you have developed or strengthened? Are there any skills you would like the opportunity to develop more in the upcoming weeks and months?*
- *What are some elements of the position you are not enjoying as much? Is this because you have not been given the proper tools or training to be successful, or because you simply do not prefer this kind of work in general?*

- *How is your onboarding going? Are there any areas where you feel you could benefit from additional support or training? So far, what part of the onboarding process has been most effective/beneficial?*

These simple questions not only can help alleviate some of the road bumps for your new hire but will also bring you a wealth of data from someone who has fresh eyes on your organization. Again, the upside is easily quantified in turnover savings and employee retention.

Fast Track to Results

To effectively recruit and retain talent:

- Make sure you clearly know what skills are prerequisite.
- Use interview questions that will highlight the candidate's skill, passion, and attitude.
- Assess unconscious biases. If you have a team that never surprises you with their questions, opinions, or insights, you do not have a diverse-enough team. Look at your organization, and assess the people who surround you.
- Pay close attention to new hires, and have processes in place to monitor and engage employees at a high level in their first 90 days. This is when they are the most vulnerable and most likely to leave.

Chapter 6

Relationships

I've never been a big "car guy." I drove a Saturn for 11 years, and it got me to my job at Disney and anywhere else I needed to go. For years, my wife, Valerie, drove a Toyota Sienna minivan, carpooling kids to various sports practices, games, and school events. It was a great car that could handle the wear and tear. One day, Valerie gave me a heads-up that her next car was going to be really nice. She had been the soccer mom for years and was now ready to be a cool mom again. As soon as our oldest son, Jullian, left for college, Valerie was in the market for a luxury SUV, and our first stop was Audi.

When we arrived at the dealership, we explained to the salesman that this was going to be my wife's car, and that I was only there as an observer and supporter. He then proceeded to talk to me about the car, the mechanical features, and everything it had to offer. When it was time to take a test drive, he handed me the keys. I wanted to tell him that there was no uncertainty that he had blown this sale. Even though I had told him to talk to my wife, he did not listen. I handed the keys to Valerie for the test drive. To make matters worse, he exclaimed, "You won't even test drive it?" We politely thanked him for his time and left. Valerie's point of view was that he could have given us the car, and she would not have taken it. She felt disrespected because he had largely ignored her during the sales process, even though I told him that it was going to be *her* car!

So, we headed to BMW, where you really get to spend your money fast! We met Hugh. As we had done at the Audi dealership, we told Hugh that this was going to be Valerie's car. He heard us loud and clear, and the sales process started. Hugh focused on Valerie, engaging in a lively conversation as he gathered information on how and when she would be using the car, what mattered to her (namely safety, intuitive tech features, and ease of maintenance), and what she needed in a car. Hugh barely looked at me during this process, and two hours later, we left the dealership having purchased a new BMW.

We drove the car home and, later that day, were surprised to receive a call from Hugh. He asked Valerie if she had taken the car for a spin and if she had any questions. As a matter of fact, Valerie was having difficulties trying to sync the remote garage door opener. Hugh immediately offered to come over and appeared at our doorstep 20 minutes later. He set the remote garage door opener feature, chatted for a while, and gave us his personal cell phone number for future questions. In the year that followed, Hugh would swing by our house to pick up the BMW for service and lend his own car to Valerie to use for the day. Now, that's service! As nice as Valerie and I are, we never thought a car salesperson would have any interest in pursuing the relationship once the deal was done. But as we continued to interact with Hugh, there were no strings attached, just genuine care from someone who understood the power of relationships.

Since that time, I have referred at least ten people to BMW, and many of them have bought cars from Hugh. Sure, you could question his motives. Is Hugh building relationships with people with the sole purpose to sell more cars? Heck, yes! He is matching his talent at relationship-building to his trade, which is selling. But aren't we all selling something every day? Even if we do not have "products" that we are trying to sell, or "sales" attached to our title, I will argue that we are absolutely selling—selling our opinions, selling our ideas, influencing others to see things the way we do, or getting others to do what needs to be done.

Now, I am not saying that we all leverage relationships every moment to get what we want. But when you are vested in a relationship and continue to build rapport, you create an auspicious environment for trust. This is true in personal and professional relationships. By showing genuine interest in people, getting to know them, and paying attention to their interests, needs, challenges, and aspirations, you foster a culture where individuals feel they matter. And when people feel they matter, they are inspired to help you or work harder and better for you. With better relationships, miscommunication goes down, and trust goes up. Everything gets easier.

Relationships are a two-way street.

Imagine you are staring down a two-way street with an outbound and inbound direction.

On the outbound, you as an individual have to be willing to show exactly who you are. By putting yourself out there and having genuine interactions, your team can see your true nature with its strengths and flaws. It makes your life easier as you do not have to pretend to be something you're not. It makes them more comfortable because they do not have to second-guess you or read between the lines every time you say something. I realize some leaders may shy away from this—*because they are afraid to be found out.* They want to project a certain image they cannot live up to, so they would rather hide behind a pretend persona or keep their distance. If there is total transparency, there is nowhere to hide! Trust me, there is no upside to playing the hiding game. Sooner or later, you will be found out, and then your credibility will be shot. So you might as well be genuine and honest with yourself and your team.

When you are vested in a relationship and continue to build rapport, you create an auspicious environment for trust.

On the inbound, you will receive valuable information that will make your work relationships a lot easier to maneuver. You will learn about *their* kingdom. First, you will quickly measure the level of candor they choose to adopt. Some folks will go all-in right away. Others may keep their cards close to their vests: perhaps they do not trust you as an individual, or they do not trust your position. Some employees have had bad experiences with their leaders in the past and may have decided to adopt a cautious approach. Depending on how much you are willing to invest in the relationship, this may change over time, and you can win these employees over. Other times, you may encounter a "yes man" who just goes through the motions. In that case, you will have to teach them to be candid. Sometimes, I would prompt some people by saying, "Thank you for agreeing with me, but please tell me why I am mistaken," or, better yet, "Thank you for being so positive but, now, please tell me why my idea sucks." Give them opportunities to show their true colors.

As I get to know people better, it provides me with indications on how they operate, what keeps them awake at night, what they hope to accomplish, and which obstacles they have to overcome. At Disney, I could also calibrate the level of empathy or recognition they required. This is all very pertinent information for building a great work relationship.

Next time you pitch an idea and people tell you it is great, respond by saying, "Thank you for the positive feedback—now tell me why my idea sucks!"

Personal relationships do not relieve you from your responsibilities.

In 2009, as a result of the economic recession and our dwindling attendance, Walt Disney World went through a round of layoffs across the top. They were cuts made unrelated to performance on a variety of positions around the parks, and we were issued a list of names by the company's HR department. I was VP of Epcot at the time and received the dreaded list for my operation. The department GMs, the Epcot HR director, and I were to deliver the news, so we went about splitting the list of names among ourselves. As fate would have it, I immediately recognized the name of a dear family friend working at Epcot. Valerie and I had known her for years and even attended her wedding in Paris. There was no doubt in my mind that I should be the one delivering the news to her. As difficult as it was, I felt she would find solace in learning her fate from someone she knew well. We had mutual respect, and I made sure she knew this was not personal nor a reflection of her abilities. I cannot imagine trying to dodge my responsibilities as a friend and a leader.

In this instance, I was dealing with someone who had been a friend *before* working in my organization, but this unusual and difficult experience taught me a valuable lesson. As you build rapport with your team, do not lose sight of the fact that one day you may have to make decisions that impact them negatively. You are in a position of authority and may have to deal with delicate situations. Your decision-making process should not be clouded by biased considerations. As a leader, there is a subtle limit to the relationships you can build with direct reports. You do not want to paint yourself into a corner where protecting a relationship comes at odds with your professional responsibility.

Build relationships with your direct reports.

While I enjoyed interacting with as many of the 12,000 cast members at the Magic Kingdom as I could, I also realized that I needed to spend much more time with my direct reports. In every organization, our direct reports are an extension of our ability in getting work done, creating the right culture for our organizations, and transmitting our values and priorities to teams. Our direct reports should be empowered with the authority to move the business forward—so a leader is only as good as his direct reports.

When I joined a new team, I would make sure to have lunch with each one of my direct reports. We would take a couple of hours to chat with no agenda. The goal of the lunch was to talk as little as possible about current work topics. I wanted to dig deeper into their personal stories: where they grew up; what jobs and experiences they had throughout their careers; and their families, passions, and personal goals. Generally, many leaders know surprisingly little about their teams, even though they spend large chunks of their day interacting with them.

These lunches gave me another level of understanding about my direct reports and what they valued. I would note the ages of their kids, whether or not their spouses worked, and what they did in their free time. This would give me the ability to later ask relevant questions about their lives and connect more effectively and authentically.

Likewise, I would always start my staff meetings by giving everyone a chance to tell a story about something exceptional that had happened recently in their professional or personal lives. These stories were entertaining, insightful, and helped the team continue to connect with each other.

I would also send out a worksheet to my team members, asking them about favorite songs, movies, food, and more. This was another source of understanding them on a personal level and enabling myself to treat them as individuals and make them feel special. Such relationship-building, I believed, also had a ripple effect: my team members would treat their colleagues—and eventually our guests—the same way. Role modeling can be powerful!

I once witnessed an executive mistake a longtime administrative assistant for a new hire and hand her a welcome basket. How can that be? How can one walk past someone's desk every day not knowing their name, much less their face? How can one expect efforts and commitment from someone they won't acknowledge? The way you interact and relate with people is crucial to building a team. Relationships are the fuel that brings energy and engagement to your organization. We live in a world where people crave human interaction and significance. Not investing in building relationships is denying them on both counts.

Build a relationship with your boss.

In 2005, I was the general manager of the All-Star Resort, the biggest hotel on Disney property. The duty manager would call me in the middle of the night if anything unusual happened. (A 5,760-room hotel has a lot of activity, shenanigans, and hijinx, but that is for another book!)

On one particular night, I was informed that an inebriated individual had pulled up to the Security gate of the All-Star. He was looking for a cast member working at the hotel and had a firearm on the passenger seat. The Security host at the gate had called law enforcement, and the man was apprehended without incident.

I proceeded to gather as much detail as I could. Who was the man in the truck? What kind of truck? What had he said? Who was the cast member in the hotel he was looking for? I soon called my boss, Kevin, to update him on the situation and shared all the details. I knew he liked details, and I was going to deliver! After I gave him the report, I took a breath and, with a sense of pride, knew that I had provided every piece of information possible. I then asked Kevin if he had any questions. He paused and then asked, "What kind of gun was it?" Sigh.

I had many leaders throughout my career at Disney. They were all different, with various levels of expectations, styles, and idiosyncrasies. As a Walt Disney GM, the first boss I had, Karl, thought fast and moved fast. Our one-on-one monthly meetings would last about 15 minutes. If I could communicate my needs in a clear, concise way in twenty words or fewer on each topic, without a lot of details, he was inclined to agree or approve my proposal on the spot. If there was any doubt in my tone, he would ask for more details. He had a high sense of urgency and liked to move at lightning pace—the type of person who's very fun to work for, but you'd better have your story straight and know how to pitch it succinctly.

My second boss, Kevin, could not have been more different. He was a master of details. He wanted a lot of specifics and to know about how projects were progressing, five percent at a time. He explained to his GMs that his need for details should not be seen as mistrust or micromanaging. He simply felt more comfortable with details, and he slept better at night when he was informed. (Remember, "What kind of gun was it?")

I had to learn how to work much differently with each boss. Some are very quick to set the ground rules. Others might keep you guessing. If no information is forthcoming, make sure to ask precisely what level of communication and what type of information they need. Over time, you should be able to understand their personalities, cater to their individual expectations, and adjust to the level of urgency and detail they require.

Fast Track to Results

How to Build Relationships with Your Direct Reports
- Spend time early in the working relationship to get to know your direct reports personally—including their background, work history, families, and hobbies.

- At the beginning of your 1–1s, engage in a personal conversation to build rapport.
- Reciprocate with your own personal information. Authenticity is a powerful tool to connect with others.
- Identify your direct reports' preferences in terms of communication, feedback, and praise. They will notice and value your personalized approach.

How to Build Relationship with Your Boss

- Align expectations quickly when working for a new boss. Ask probing questions on deadlines, the amount of communication they prefer, and what they consider "urgent."
- Cover items important to their job; offer thoughts about your current projects; and humble brag about some of your great work they may not know about.
- Make it easy for your boss to give you feedback, acknowledging areas that you need to improve upon.

Chapter 7

Setting Expectations

Here is a classic story. Mom tells teenager, "Honey, don't come back home too late!" Teenager gets back home at midnight and gets car privileges revoked because he was expected by 10 P.M. Teenager exclaims: "Mom, that's not fair—midnight isn't late at all! I can't believe you're taking my car away just for that!"

Dear Mom, I'm afraid the joke is on you. The lack of clear expectations left room for interpretation. "Not too late" is vague, so the teenager translated the expectation into his own terms. When we don't determine the boundaries and consequences in advance, we create ambiguity. And ambiguity opens the door to misinterpretation, which generates confusion and frustration.

Over the years, I have often heard myself say, "Can you please get back to me on this issue?" only to get frustrated when the information was not forthcoming the next day. Again, by failing to give a precise deadline,

I did not convey any level of urgency and left my team guessing.

Other times, I had team members *over*deliver. In 2002, I was the general manager of the Wilderness Lodge. While chatting with the restaurant's chef, I mentioned casually how fun it would be to have kids make gingerbread houses for the holidays. About a week later, the Food and Beverage manager for the hotel asked me why she had not been told about my Gingerbread House Initiative.

I was initially baffled but soon realized that what I had considered just a passing remark had been taken at face value. The chef had ordered the supplies and had rearranged the schedule to put the plan in place, much to the surprise of his direct leader. He assumed my "brainstorming" was an order he needed to follow immediately. This could not have been further from the truth but, again, my lack of clarity had left the door wide open for interpretation.

We can easily correct this kind of confusion. Don't keep people guessing. Be specific with deadlines, and set clear parameters and goals—particularly when you step into a new organization.

Operating Practices and Priorities

Starting a new job or shifting within the company typically includes a period of trial and error. A team member does something out of line with the leader's thinking or misreads the signals. There is a correction, and then the team adjusts and moves on. But as a result, trust and understanding take longer to build, and all the while, productivity suffers during this period of uncertainty.

My goal from day one was to avoid such mishaps and accelerate the learning curve. I needed to share how I processed information, how I expected communication to flow, and generally how to best work with me. I recognized an opportunity to accelerate the learning curve in stating formally and precisely what was on my mind and not making my team guess whether I operated like their previous leader.

I discovered a foolproof way to create such clarity.

Wait for it ...

I *wrote down* my expectations and gave them to my team. Imagine that! I called the document "Dan's Operating Practices and Priorities." (See the full memo at DanCockerell.com/expectations.)

This was a living, breathing document that evolved over decades. Each time I went into a new job, I would fine-tune my expectations based on my learnings and newly found wisdom from the last job. Your own expectations will look different according to your leadership style and company culture. But a similar document will give you a good foundation.

Now, just because I wrote everything on a piece of paper and gave it to my team did not mean that we had established trust, nor that the future was going to be all rainbows and ponies! That would only come with time and experience together. This type of memo, however, is an effective tool to take a lot of the guesswork out of the first 6-12 months with a new team. It helps create a faster path to trust and productivity.

Here are some of the key themes from that document.

On Leadership:

What is your leadership philosophy? What do you want your direct reports to know about what you value as a leader? In my case, I discuss the four pillars that guide my leadership style:

- The importance of leveraging everyone's talent
- Building strong relationships
- Setting clear expectations
- Reward/recognition

On Communication:

What do you consider great communication? How do you prefer to be communicated to and with what frequency? What level of detail do you prefer? What will be the frequency and structure of your team meetings and 1–1s with your team? How should they expect you to communicate with them?

On Problem-Solving:

Define the level of empowerment, freedom, and support you will provide your team to solve problems. Do you expect them to come to you only when they have exhausted every other option? Would you like them to use you as a thought partner? How much risk do you want them to take in performing their roles? What are the criteria you would like them to use when making decisions?

On Development:

What role will you play for your direct reports' ongoing development? Will you present a plan to them? Will you put the responsibility on them to identify their areas of opportunity and work with you to develop a plan? How much time, resources, and money are you willing to invest in their development? This area is important to define. A motivated, high-performing leader has a keen interest in team members' development.

On Performance:

Where will you set the bar for your team? If you set it too low, you will leave value on the table. Too high, and they may see your vision as unattainable. Aim for the Goldilocks zone—just right. How much do you value relationships versus results? What are the most important metrics you will use to measure their performance? Will you use their team's feedback about them in your assessment?

Folded into the performance expectations part of your memo should also be a section about balance and how you think about it. Is there a minimum amount of hours you expect your team to work every week? Do you expect your team to be available seven days a week? After hours? On vacation? Do you expect them to deputize one of their team members when they are not available to represent them? (This was a key tactic at Disney, open 365 days a year.) When the time came for annual performance evaluations, I could easily pull up my Operating Practices and Priorities. Holding people accountable is a lot easier when you have clearly stated your expectations.

Understanding Expectations

I am a big proponent of servant leadership. This means leaders should consider their main responsibility to be supporting their team members. As mentioned earlier, much like a coach, you select the team members; you train them; you provide them with tools, practices, and strategy; you support and encourage them—and they're off to do the job.

In order to be effective and bring them the support they need, it is important to start asking questions.

A very effective way to get the right answers to these questions is a "Start, Stop, Continue" session. At Walt Disney World, top leaders perform this exercise once or twice a year.

Here is how it plays out.

Take your team out for a morning or afternoon, and gather them in a casual setting away from their regular work location. Let them know that you are committed to their success, and since you are here to help them, you need to know what they expect from their leader. Explain that there are things you do well and things you need to work on, and you welcome their feedback.

Put up three flip charts. Tell the team you will leave for 90 minutes in order for the group to discuss what they think should go under each rubric: start doing, stop doing, and continue doing. They should also prioritize each list. You may enlist the help of a neutral moderator to engage the team and facilitate the input while you step away. (This person can be from HR or someone who has no skin in the game). Before you return, the team can nominate a spokesperson or two.

Listen intently to the feedback.

Once you have heard the feedback, ask questions to make sure you understand the intent and context of the group's thoughts. This is important since you will be creating an action plan and sharing it with them. Take away your thoughts and notes from the meeting and, within a week, send your notes to the team or review with them the steps you are going to take.

The advantages of this exercise are twofold. First, you will be more likely to get honest feedback from the group since there is strength and safety in numbers. Nobody has to put themselves at risk—the feedback is presented on behalf of the group.

It also sends a strong message that you value continuous improvement and that you are willing to be vulnerable enough to allow a conversation about your own performance. This is very difficult, and always stings a bit when you hear some of the feedback. However, the impact can be spectacular.

It is important to remember that this is a two-way process, and if you have additional thoughts about why you do what you do, or there are certain things that you will not change, be sure to explain why. Sometimes just discussing an issue will be enough action.

Lastly, before undertaking this process, be sure you are willing to make an action plan and follow through. Commit to less than you think you should, and make sure you complete the requested changes. It is better to never have the meeting at all than to have it and lose credibility by not following through.

Silent Leadership—the Power of Role Modeling

As I prepared the different topics for this book, I initially omitted role modeling. It was a deliberate choice as I felt it transpired through much of the content already. Besides, role modeling is rooted in our DNA. This is how we acquire most of our basic skills and should therefore be the easiest thing to remember and put into practice. Think about it for a second: we basically learn how to stand, walk, and talk through our parents' role modeling. We adopt values, traits, and behaviors through role modeling.

We get inspired, motivated, and empowered through role modeling. We learn, evolve, and improve thanks to role modeling.

Role modeling is not only vital to creating the right culture for an organization but also the easiest way to create standard behaviors, communicate what is important, and train and motivate people. It is *the most important element* of leadership excellence.

So, on second thought, I decided to share another story that showcases the power of role modeling and its impact.

Back in 2014, I was VP of Disney's Hollywood Studios, and we were approaching the end of the year and another busy holiday season. The Studios have always been a destination of choice during Christmas because of the Festival of Lights. This particular year was going to be challenging because of insufficient parking facilities for the forecasted attendance. To free up some valuable parking space for our guests, I decided to ask the Studios' cast members to park in a remote location (the ESPN Wide World of Sports), and we organized shuttles to and from work. This added an extra thirty minutes to their everyday commute—needless to say, many cast members were unhappy with the decision.

As soon as we made the announcement, several of the cast members gathered the courage to call me directly and protest the new arrangements. I would let them vent for a good five minutes, thank them for their call, and tell them I understood *precisely* how this impacted them since we all shared the same circumstances. When I decided to request remote parking, I insisted the entire leadership team, myself included, adhere to the same requirements. Even though my office was immediately in the backstage area, where we had about twenty parking spots reserved for our own coming and going, all the leaders made a point of riding the shuttle with the frontline cast members as a show of solidarity.

It was a hassle for all of us, and we could have easily made an exception for the executives, but I knew that this was exactly the type of scenario that would make or break our reputation. If, as a leader, I am to request my team to make an extra effort, I must set the example and be right there with them. And let me tell you, people watch you—*all the time.* They listen to you and, more importantly, observe what you do and how you behave. Based on these observations, they determine what is important to you and will emulate your behavior, good or bad. If you talk to people about safety and drive like a maniac, clearly safety isn't important to you, and therefore not important to them. If you talk about being truthful, and your kids catch you lying, you can bet they will also lie at one point or another. Role modeling is as important to leadership as it is to parenting.

So as you build expectations for your team, do remember that nothing will be more important than your own behaviors. They tell the story of what is important to you, how much you care about your team, and whether you are true to your word.

Fast Track to Results

Here are some key insights on expectations:

- Create your own expectations memo to share with your direct reports. Set aside a notebook that you will use for fine-tuning this memo over time. (You can see some ideas from my own Operating Practices and Priorities at DanCockerell.com/Resources.) In this memo, describe your philosophy on key themes, such as these:
  - Leadership
  - Communication
  - Problem-Solving
  - Development
  - Performance
- Host a Stop, Start, Continue session. Follow through with an action plan.
- Always role model your expectations.

Chapter 8

Reward and Recognition

In the drawer of my desk at Disney, I kept what I called the "You did good!" folder. When I made a mistake or a bad decision, or simply had a rough day, I'd pull out this folder. It was full of thank-you notes, congratulations from my boss, letters from cast members and guests telling me about something magical that I did for them, and more. The "You did good!" folder was my therapy to get through challenging times when I started second-guessing myself. I cannot speak on behalf of all the executives, but believe me when I say that most of them have moments of insecurity and anxiety just like everyone else. Those little pieces of paper propped me back up.

Similarly, I met many cast members who still kept some of the cards or notes I had written them years before. These mementos were words of appreciation for a project well done, an encouragement for continuous efforts, or a thank-you for consistently displaying great behaviors. Some kept them in their desks and others in their wallets; one cast member even had one of my notes framed in his living room. Who knew these little pieces of paper had so much value? Napoleon Bonaparte once said, "A soldier will fight long and hard for a bit of colored ribbon." I'll second that!

The Power of Reward and Recognition

Knowing the power of reward and recognition (and its effect on me) inspired me to put the right tools and processes in place to make sure plenty of recognition was happening in each of my organizations.

At speaking engagements nowadays, I often ask audiences why they think we should recognize and reward people's performance. I get lots of absolutely reasonable responses: to motivate people, to make them feel good, to let them know we appreciate them. These are all certainly outcomes, but I like to think of recognition as a leadership tool to reinforce individual behaviors (which creates culture) and motivate teams to be more productive for the organization as a whole.

For example, if I saw an employee consistently going out of his way to greet each customer as they entered a merchandise location, it was perfectly reasonable and necessary to tell that employee that I noticed they were greeting each guest, and that I valued that behavior. Once I did so, it was reasonable to believe that the employee was going to continue that behavior. If I wanted the cast member to be safe, I needed to look for manifested efforts to create a safe environment. If I wanted the cast member to be courteous, my comments needed to focus on specific behaviors when the team member was being particularly helpful and respectful, creating magical moments, and going above and beyond... I think you get the idea.

At Disney, I reviewed guest letters, emails, and social media posts, and I insisted that any compliment letter identifying a specific cast member would be forwarded to him or her with a handwritten thank-you note from me. It seemed appropriate to let them know and show some appreciation. Employees matter, and they need to know they matter. In my later years at Disney, and at the Magic Kingdom in particular, my assistant, Kathleen, would help me by typing up notes for me to sign. The volume of compliment letters was too big to handle myself. That was one of my favorite "problems" to be confronted with!

Types of Recognition

At Disney, I also learned how to think about spontaneous recognition versus program-driven recognition. I believe that there is a place for programs such as employee of the month, performance- or attendance-based recognition. However, we need to make sure the criteria are extremely clear and understood by everyone in the organization. I also found over the years that "award" programs involving peer recognition carried more weight among our team, provided of course that it recognized the appropriate behaviors.

The most important thing I learned was that every recognition program has a shelf life. Sometimes weeks, sometimes months. It is perfectly fine to change up the programs, as long as you focus on reinforcing behaviors that you expect from your teams. Do not let them grow stale, or the programs lose all credibility.

Spontaneous recognition, meanwhile, creates an element of surprise that can increase motivation and make coming into work more fun for the recipient and the contributor. It has to happen in the moment, and obviously implies that you witness the behavior. Sometimes a simple "Thank you" will suffice, be it verbally or via text or email. But the more immediate, the more effective it will be.

It takes discipline to get into the habit of showing appreciation because we are caught up in the moment, and urgent matters often push recognition to the back burners. You see the behaviors; you witness the behaviors; you intend to acknowledge the employee but never get around to doing it. Before you know it, the time has passed, and it's over and forgotten.

My wife often mentioned how challenging it was for her to remember to provide recognition. It may have been a cultural difference (more on that later) as French people are not "natural cheerleaders," so she developed a system. I am not sure where she heard or read about this, but here is how it played out: Valerie would put five coins in her right pocket every morning. The idea was that the jingling coins would remind her to be looking for great team members, peers, or partners, and recognize and thank them on the spot. Every time she did so, she would move one coin to her left pocket. She aimed to put all five coins in her left pocket by the end of the day, thus ensuring that she had thanked and encouraged at least five people that day. The first week or so was tough, and she would often return home with her stash of coins still tucked into the right pocket, but over time, she gradually became more diligent and vocal about recognition. Et voilá!

This is an area where we can be as creative as we want, either by devising our own system (like Valerie did) or making the recognition moment fun and imaginative. Rachel, the general manager of Entertainment at the Magic Kingdom, would bring the cast members she wanted to praise into her weekly staff meetings. She would read a letter about something great the cast member had done, and her team would conclude with a standing ovation. In her Merchandise department, Deb would create small candy packs with Lifesavers inside. As she walked the park, she'd reward great customer service moments in real time. Personally, I have baked quite a few banana breads that I would hand out to random high performers I came across during my day. It became known as a Danana Bread, and I surprised many a cast member over the years. Now, I am not implying that you should start baking away, but a simple gesture goes a long way. Besides, I like to think it is good karma.

Nothing bad can happen to you when you start the day handing out homemade bread!

One more note: as mentioned earlier, I believe we should approach our lives holistically. We do not have a personal life and a professional life—we have one life. This goes for our team members, too. When the going got tough and the team had to work extra long hours, I was very well aware of the fact that this was time taken away from their families. Therefore, I always made a point of acknowledging their spouses or kids, who were the ones affected the most by their absence. After the busy Christmas season, I would send dinner coupons to the spouses and partners of the team members and thank them for sharing their spouse/partner with our organization. This was a simple way to give them some quality time back.

No One-Size-Fits-All for Rewards and Recognition Programs

While working with the opening team at Disneyland Paris, I started a "perfect attendance" program for the Parking Operation team. In the breakroom, cast members who had not called in sick or missed work would have their names posted on a list in the breakroom for "two weeks perfect attendance," "one month perfect attendance," and so on.

When we reached a couple of months into the program, one sole cast member was left with perfect attendance. He took me aside one day and explained that he appreciated the recognition, but the other cast members were really giving him a hard time about "being better than them." He told me that if I did not take the list down, he would have to call in sick in order to get his name off the board. I discontinued the perfect attendance program immediately. What an interesting learning regarding cultural differences! This program had worked perfectly well at Walt Disney World. I learned that generally, French individuals would much rather be recognized in a private way, which is why the perfect-at-tendance Parking cast member felt uncomfortable.

Meanwhile, in the US, it's a different story, at least from my experience. When recognizing an American employee, be sure to have balloons, some sort of sign and, if possible, their friends and family invited. There will be speeches, peers will chime in, and much backslapping will take place. I may be exaggerating a bit, but there is a lot of truth to these cultural differences. And by the way, that is exactly what they are: differences. Not better, not worse, just different.

To avoid stepping out of line, ask your individual team members how they like to be recognized. Some will say in private and some will say in public. Some will tell you that peace of mind is their recognition, and to regularly let them know they are doing good work. But others will tell you that talk is cheap and that they want you to put your money where your mouth is. Whatever you do, do something! Traditionally, reward and recognition programs receive the lowest ratings on employee surveys. We did a very good job at Disney with a variety of programs and awards, and this was still one of our lowest-rated areas of leadership. So, treat reward and recognition just like you do any other business metric. Put the processes in place to make sure it happens, be careful to tailor it to the individual, and ensure that it reinforces the behaviors expected in your organization.

Individuals vs. Teams

Organizations get results in two different ways: individual performance and team performance. During my career, maintaining the balance of supporting both was always a dilemma. The behaviors we encourage and reward are the behaviors we get. The grid on the next page lays out the resulting dynamics of each environment.

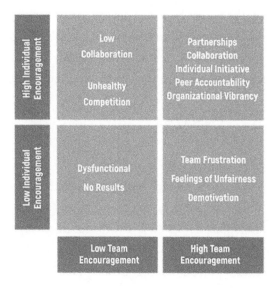

Leaders who evaluate their teams mostly on individual performance miss out on their direct reports helping each other solve issues as a group.

When we overvalue individual behavior, each person is focused on how to get noticed and prove their worth to their boss. People do not "watch each other's back" and may allow another team member to fail so that, comparatively, they are seen as a high achiever.

On the other hand, leaders who evaluate their team mostly on team performance also put results at risk. On any team, there will be trailblazers who can contribute more value. However, if their individual efforts are not recognized or rewarded, they are likely to pull back or leave the organization.

The reality is that we need both. Today's world is too complex and fast moving for any one individual to get it all done. We need everyone's point of view, knowledge, wisdom, and contribution for the team to be successful. The power lies in the team.

We also need individual talent to move the team forward but not to become the only star.

Tom Staggs, the former chairman of Disney Parks and Resorts, called it "organizational vibrancy." The concept is simple. As a leader, you're expected to perform at an excellent level individually and simultaneously make those around you better through partnering and collaboration.

Fast Track to Results

Providing the right recognition implies that:
- You are familiar with each individual's preference for recognition: private vs. public, written vs. oral, etc.
- You find opportunities every day to recognize employees for their performance and achievements, big or small.
- You create a process to recognize and reward. It is not a behavior that comes naturally for many.
- You consider a mix of structured and spontaneous reward and recognition.
- You always connect reward and recognition to your formal expectations in order to reinforce what you value.

Chapter 9:

Giving Effective Feedback

aris, 1993. I was about one year into my stint at Disneyland Paris and had reached a much-dreaded professional milestone: firing my first cast member. This particular individual, whom I will refer to as Jean-Pierre, had been a poor performer for a while, and the day had come for me to deliver the news. As he arrived at work, I asked him to come by my office, and we both sat down. I proceeded to painstakingly explain the reason why I had made that decision. It was an uncomfortable moment (at best), and it took me a while to get to the point, namely that his career at Disney was over. There was much contorting on my part, partly because of my still-burgeoning mastery of French, but mainly because I was generally unprepared. The conversation ended. Jean-Pierre left. I breathed a sigh of relief and went on with my day—only to find out that after our conversation, Jean-Pierre had returned to his position in the parking lot! Clearly, my feedback had not "landed!" (More on that word later in this chapter.)

Early on in my career, I really struggled with similar situations and, more generally, with providing difficult feedback. I would get nervous, with knots in my stomach and anxiety building up until, at last, I had to provide the feedback or drop the verdict. It often left a bitter taste in my mouth as I knew I was not handling it very well.

Why do we avoid giving negative feedback?

- We're scared.
- We don't want to damage the relationship.
- We worry about the other person's reaction or feelings.
- We are not sure how to say it.
- We don't know all the facts.
- We have never told them before.

The list goes on.

However, feedback is a prerequisite for teams to succeed. So, I started to read about it, talked to people, and observed others with more experience. I also reflected on my own feelings when someone gave me feedback and how I reacted to it.

I was immediately drawn to the concept of "notes" (which sounds so much more positive than "feedback"). If you happen to work in the entertainment industry, whether you're a performer, dancer, or singer, the director of the show will usually approach you after your performance and give you notes. These notes may be ranging from "You should kick higher" or "Smile more" or "You didn't quite hit the right note" or "You need to get over to this side of the stage more quickly." The entertainment cast members are accustomed to feedback and expect it. It's not considered a performance review but just "real-time" feedback. It is understood as part of the job: *I'm getting notes because I'm performing. There's always something I can do better, and the director is there to help me do that.* In the entertainment industry, feedback is a consistent and legitimate part of the culture. How do we replicate this in our organizations? How can we create a culture of positivity around feedback—even negative feedback—by making it a regular, routine occurrence instead of doomsday?

What We Are Fighting

First, much of today's workforce was raised on positive feedback regardless of performance. If you have ever sat on the sidelines of a youth sport event, you surely will understand what I am talking about. It is all positive, all the time. No wonder so many people have a tough time accepting any negative feedback—they've never heard it before.

If you grew up with "helicopter parents" or "snowplow" parents—who will not only oversee everything their kids do, but also remove all obstacles—you, too, would have a hard time receiving feedback or being on the losing end of a decision. I once met with a 23-year-old college program employee who was astounded that she had not been selected to become a Disney Trainer (one step up from a frontline role). I pointed out that it was okay, as she was still new to the company and learning. Her response? "You don't understand. I have never failed at anything before!"

Another pitfall of our culture is that we too often celebrate results instead of effort. We often look at positive outcomes as the only criteria for success. As I discussed in Chapter 2 on mental fitness, we too often look upon failure as shameful. So people get defensive, do not see the opportunity for growth in receiving negative feedback, ignore it, and continue on with the same behavior. Isn't the definition of insanity doing the same thing over and over again while expecting different results?

Finally, because of our discomfort in providing feedback, we often drag our feet and delay the inevitable. One thing to remember: "In feedback, silence fails!" The longer we wait, the harder it will be to give *and* receive. If we do not address poor performance immediately, an employee will believe this behavior is acceptable and continue the fairy tale. Before we know it, others will emulate the same behaviors and poison the well.

This is how organizational culture surreptitiously erodes: certain behaviors are unacceptable, then become "frowned upon," eventually are "tolerated," and one day are deemed admissible and common practice.

Regardless, it is our job as leaders to create an environment where feedback is continuous, accepted, and valued. If we are going to work to get better and operate in a high-performance organization, there is no way around it. Call it feedback, notes, or whatever, but this is the lifeblood of continuous improvement.

How to Give Successful Feedback

Before Delivering Feedback

By having a plan in place, we can remain rational when the emotions of giving feedback kick in and the amygdala part of our brain triggers our fight-or-flight response. A plan ensures we can continue to have a high quality, logical, and effective conversation.

Ask yourself these three questions:

What is the quality of this relationship? One afternoon, I was "walking the park" with my HR manager and came across a merchandise cast member named Jim essentially hiding behind his cart. I approached him and gave him some very clear instructions. "Good afternoon, Jim," I said. "Can you please get your butt out here and talk to some of these nice guests who are paying so much money to see your beautiful smile?"

Jim smiled and came out in front of the cart. "Sorry Dan, was slacking off a bit there," he said.

My HR manager stopped me with a concerned look on his face. "Dan, you can't say that to a cast member! It is disrespectful, and you can't tell him to move his 'butt!'" He was right. But he did not know I had met Jim 20 years earlier in a previous area, and we had a trusting relationship. He was one of my listening posts—someone on the front line who would tell me the word on the street. Jim was a good cast member, and we had a mutual respect. A few weeks before this very day, he had actually told *me* I should get out of my "ivory tower" and get *my* butt into the park where the action was. This was the level at which we communicated with one another. Obviously, that is not something I could have done with just anyone. I had adjusted my comment based on our level of interaction.

The same was true for my direct reports. I had a unique mutual understanding with each of them. The comfort and trust factor were extremely high with some and average with others. So I always assessed the relationship quality beforehand to help me determine my style of feedback. To help in this process, think about the level of trust that you have for each other and whether the employee will assume you have good or bad intentions. Ask yourself whether you have had similar conversations before and if there is any chance the employee may think it is personal. Overall, thinking through the different approaches and possible reactions and having clear talking points will prevent the conversation from getting awkward.

What expectations have I set? It is important to examine how we have communicated expectations on the particular issue we are about to address. It does not mean that we will change our feedback, but I have found that when I think deeply about the expectations I have set—or not set—I can better modulate the feedback. Unless this is a recurring issue, we don't want to find ourselves saying, "You should have known." Our responsibility as leaders is to make sure that we create clarity of expectations in our organization so our teams don't have to guess what is acceptable and unacceptable.

What will happen if I do not provide this feedback? I always think about the consequences of not providing the feedback. Over time, if we do not deal with issues head-on, we lose credibility (and eventually our ability to lead); our operation becomes less efficient or productive; and our organizational culture weakens. If we are passionate and serious about our job, then we must summon up the courage to directly address issues. Because if we don't do our job, the organization will hire someone else who will!

While Delivering Feedback

First, keep in mind that feedback is about behavior, not character. You may not approve of someone's behavior, but that does not make them a bad person—just someone who made a bad choice or acted inappropriately. This is not a life judgment, and it does not "define" the person. That person stepped out of line. You are here to help correct their course.

Second, find the right voice. We make mistakes in coming on too harsh or too meek. Just like Goldilocks, you have to find what is "just right." Get the emotions out of the way. Sleep on it if you have to. Wait until the adrenaline stops pumping and be careful with your wording and tone of voice.

Let's look at three different scenarios and the different possible approaches—"too soft," "too hard," and "just right."

Someone is consistently late.

- Too soft: "I know that you have a lot going on ..."
- Too hard: "You're always late; what is your problem?"
- Just right: "I have noticed that you are consistently late for our conference calls. Have you noticed that?"

Someone is often interrupting others.

- Too soft: "You always have a great point of view in meetings, but ..."
- Too hard: "You are always interrupting in meetings."
- Just right: "I have been watching the flow of our meetings recently, and noticed that you often interrupt others. Have you noticed that?"

Someone uses sarcasm.

- Too soft: "I think you have a great sense of humor, but ..."
- Too hard: "Did you realize that your sarcasm is not funny?"
- Just right: "I have noticed that at times you respond with humor that sounds like sarcasm to me, and I am not sure how to take it."

Finding the right voice and tone takes time and preparation, but we get better at it with practice, and it eventually becomes easier.

Third, get the facts right. If you can't support your comments with specifics, you have no credibility. Collecting data is easy enough when it is based on clearly measurable criteria such as attendance or sales. In leadership roles, however, issues can be more subjective and therefore more difficult. So be diligent, and always document all the mishaps you witness, big or small, consequential or not. Whatever the size, you will soon identify the trend. And when the trend is clear, it is time to dive into the gritty details of that particular department to find out where the breakdown is happening. The key is to document everything, no matter how insignificant it may seem initially.

Fourth, make sure the feedback has "landed." People need to listen, understand it, accept it, and actually change their behavior. That is why we are giving it in the first place! So give them time to process, and help them work through the different stages of internalization. Make sure they understand the implications and consequences of their behaviors. Watch their verbal response, body language, and tone of voice. Give them a chance to answer and provide clarification if needed. The idea here is to make sure you are communicating on the same wavelength—unlike my first experience with the French cast member in Parking.

Finally, offer some words of advice. Help them get better. Isn't that the point anyway? Make sure the future expectations (and possible consequences) are understood; ask the individual to submit an action plan. The onus should be on him or her to correct course. Offer some additional training and role modeling with you or a peer if necessary.

After Delivering Feedback

Just when you thought you were done, you realize a whole lot more needs to happen. You may have delivered the message, but the next few days (or weeks) will tell if you have done so successfully. You are now hoping to see the behavioral change you discussed. So, make a note on your calendar to remind you of your to-do items:

- Monitor your employee post-feedback.
- Provide the training that you have agreed upon (if applicable).
- Share positive comments if the behavior indeed changes—or move on to the next step if there is no change to the employee's performance.

There may be a second conversation, a documented discussion, or a memo to file. The process must be fair and progressive to give the person a chance to change, but a change in behavior *must* occur. If that does not happen, eventually, termination will be the right solution.

By the way, just in case you are wondering: On that dreadful day in Paris in 1993, I went back to the parking lot to get Jean-Pierre. I brought him back to my office and this time delivered the verdict in no uncertain terms: "*Vous êtes viré* (You are fired)." Using the correct French terms, I supported the verdict with the appropriate documented reasons, and marched him off to the Administrative Office so he would turn in his Disney ID and clean out his locker. Live and learn!

Fast Track to Results

For constructive and effective feedback:

- Prepare notes and anticipate reaction based on what you know about their personality and the level of trust you share.
- Make feedback normal, not a performance review.
- Ask yourself: *What is the quality of our relationship? What expectations have I set? What will happen if I don't deliver the feedback?*
- Find the right voice, get the facts right, and ensure the feedback has landed.
- Follow through post-feedback.

Part 3:

LEADING AN ORGANIZATION

hen Walt Disney World opened in October 1971, it put Orlando on the map as a vacation destination. SeaWorld was quick to follow in 1973, and then Universal Orlando came seventeen years later. Orlando became the busiest multi-park destination in the country, and the three companies were vying for bookings and tourism dollars. Walt Disney World attracted the majority of tourists, but both Universal and SeaWorld were nipping at Disney's heels.

With this in mind, we did not get complacent. Instead, we started to look at our business model to figure out how we could differentiate ourselves from the competition. Clearly our guests were telling us that they loved our parks and resorts, but one of the chief complaints was the hassle of getting to and from our resort. What if there was a way to alleviate this issue? How could we make it easier for our guests? This is how Disney's Magical Express came to be. Starting in 2005, we offered our resort guests complimentary transportation to and from the Orlando airport as well as luggage delivery to their hotel rooms. We sent them luggage tags for their bags prior to departure. After they checked in their suitcases at their home airport, the luggage would "magically" find its way directly to their Disney hotel rooms. A motor coach was awaiting the guests at the airport to "whisk them away" to our resorts with no suitcases to worry about.

This was a huge endeavor for Disney and an ambitious way to outclass the competition. Clearly, the shrewd individuals behind this idea had anticipated that guests would flock to this service, thus bypassing car rentals. Without a car at their disposal, guests were more inclined to stay at Disney, eat at Disney, and spend their vacation dollars at Disney.

A dedicated team had been working on this initiative for about a year. The original plan was to roll this out in waves, initially excluding the All-Star Resort (a value hotel) of which I was the general manager. However, just three months before the rollout date, Disney decided to expand this offering propertywide. My team and I had to jump on the bandwagon with little notice.

As the motel-style All-Star Resort stretches a mile and offers six times more rooms than the next biggest hotel on Disney property, it presented a whole new range of logistic challenges. We had to prepare to process and deliver luggage to up to 5,760 rooms, covering significant distances and coping with weather-related issues.

I gathered the team, and we got straight to work. First, we had to ensure all cast members at the resort understood the benefit of Disney's Magical Express. We had to "sell them" on the vision and keep them aware of the upside for the guests and, ultimately, for the organization. In other words, we had to inspire and galvanize the troops while addressing the unique challenges of the All-Star layout. We created processes based on the data from Disney's Industrial Engineering Department. We hired the additional staffing to handle the luggage delivery. We trained the Front Desk and Housekeeping cast members as they would be directly impacted. We ordered all supplies including golf and luggage carts, and scanners for the tags. We prepared our call center to handle questions and possible missing luggage and worked to integrate communication among Housekeeping, Front Desk, and the delivery crew.

All leaders, including myself, put on costumes and helped out in the operation for the first couple of weeks. We wanted to see firsthand how the plan played out. I have to say that it worked pretty well considering that, with an average of three pieces of luggage per room, the All-Star moved roughly 17,000 bags or suitcases per day, effectively putting us in comparable numbers with the biggest regional airports in the US. Still, at 99.9% accuracy, we would be missing seventeen bags at the end of each day. Not something we looked forward to. So the stakes were high! We monitored each day's output and addressed issues immediately. We conducted post-rollout debriefs and fine-tuned the operation until it became fully integrated.

The Magical Express initiative was a huge success for Disney and for the All-Star. It wasn't long until our competitors felt the impact. Meanwhile our attendance and length of stay increased and our guest satisfaction surveys improved to new heights.

This is where Disney and other successful companies clearly stand out from the rest of the pack: They demonstrate *the will to always get better*. They consistently improve upon an already top-performing organization while setting a new vision and new goals for the employees. Because of Walt Disney World's size, every endeavor requires complex procedures and intensive training, a lot of creative thinking, and great communication. Moreover, these new initiatives would not be successful if Disney cast members did not operate within a clear framework empowering them to take initiative and make decisions. Through many such projects during the years, I learned firsthand that all these elements are indispensable to creating great culture and leading an organization to successful and sustainable results.

Chapter 10

Organizational Vision

W hether you lead a team, a project, a department, or an entire organization, an ambitious goal should be in your not-so-distant future. Are you striving to become the leader of your industry? Successfully commercialize a new product? Reach sales objectives? Establish your brand in new markets? Recruit and train a new team? Regardless of the scope of your responsibilities, a vision should stand as an ambitious destination for you and your team, something to work toward that will yield your strategy. Every decision made should be geared toward moving a step in that direction and bringing you closer to that goal.

It is your responsibility as a leader to define this vision and make it vibrant and dynamic, not just a dusty framed quotation on the wall. The vision is also a motivation factor for your team, something that tugs at their sense of pride and lets them foresee the future possibilities.

Here are a few things to consider.

Keep your vision simple and memorable.

When we talk about vision, it's easy to feel overwhelmed by the stories of past and current visionaries: Steve Jobs, Katherine Graham, Mark Zuckerberg, John Rockefeller, and Walt Disney, to name a few. All of them transcended their industries and left legacies for the history books. They all came up with a revolutionary product, concept, or endeavor, and challenged an entire industry in the process.

Needless to say, it is tough to measure up to transcendent leaders like these. But no need to panic. More often than not, your organization's vision should be simple and define a clear path to success. Sometimes it just means "doing well what we do best." At Disney, our Safety Department's vision was "No one gets hurt"—talk about a lofty goal! Not exactly something revolutionary rocking the Safety Department's world on its axis, but a lofty goal nonetheless. More importantly, this type of vision presents a clear path to work toward and remember.

Make it part of your decision-making.

In 2013, we rolled out My Magic Plus at Walt Disney World. This new digital reservation system allowed us to consolidate hotel-room keys, payments, and ticketing into a single wearable RFID wristband. We shipped the wristbands—which were encrypted with their park tickets, FastPasses, reservations, and more—to the guests immediately after they made their reservation. It was a big leap for Disney, to the tune of $1 billion. The *modus operandi* for the initiative was simple: "The guests better love it! The cast better love it! It better work!" In other words, "Let's make sure that it is not too complex for the guests or the cast to operate, and that whatever technology we put out there is tried and tested." With this in mind, we were able to iron out a lot of issues and shorten the learning curve for everyone. When we had to create new processes, we always asked ourselves: "Will the guests love it?" "Will the cast love it?" and "Great idea, but can we make it work?"

This may sound like a no-brainer, but every decision in your organization should move you a little closer to your vision. Too often, we lose track of why we are in business to start with or what we are trying to accomplish, especially when things get very complex or span a long period of time. We come up with new initiatives or processes that are counter to our ultimate goals. We create barriers and constraints hampering our ability to grow our business, or preventing our teams from working to the best of their capability. The bigger the organization, the more susceptible we are to deviate from our initial objectives. I can think of many examples of useless administrative tasks, contorted processes, and unnecessary approval requirements slowing us down or, worse yet, moving us farther away from the desired outcome.

So keep your vision on the front burner and top of mind in every decision you make.

Turn your vision into a common purpose.

The Walt Disney Company's vision was once to be "the most admired entertainment company in the world." As if this wasn't lofty enough, Bob Iger set the bar even higher by stating that Disney wanted to become "the most admired *company* in the world." Period.

As was the case at Disney, the overarching vision is often the brainchild of a group of executives who pursue that goal when they lay out the strategic plan for the next five to ten years. It sounds ambitious, and surely most employees will take pride in working for such an organization, especially when it has a brand recognition right up there with Coca-Cola and Apple. However, I can't help but wonder how many cast members jump out of bed in the morning proclaiming, "I am working on making Disney the most admired company in the world!" Other than the upper tier of executives, does anyone really find inspiration from this?

Hard to do when you have little direct impact. If you are the CEO and decide to donate $1 million to the recovery efforts in Haiti, give free tuition to hourly cast members, or commit to hiring 10,000 veterans, it makes the front page of the newspapers. Consequently, Disney's star shines a little brighter and the company becomes a little more laudable every time.

But what to make of the frontline cast members who run the attractions, prepare and serve food, or clean hotel rooms? Are they working toward making Disney the most admired company in the world? Of course they are, but it is harder for the front-line employees to see how they contribute to that. They, too, make a difference, and as leaders, we need to guide and spur them along by providing them with a more concrete goal. They need *a common purpose*. It's far more effective to assign them an objective that lies within their reach and can motivate them to go above and beyond their job responsibilities on a *day-to-day basis*. Give them something they can impact personally and directly and that bears fruit immediately. Because it is more attainable, employees can rally around it, take ownership, and find gratification. *The common purpose shows how and why they influence and impact your organization's success.* All employees matter and need to know they matter.

You must provide your team with a tangible target, an objective that motivates them to go above and beyond their job responsibilities on *a day-to-day basis.*

At Disney, cast members make magic! Through all their interactions, they contribute to making memorable guest experiences, which in turn grow the organization's reputation for excellence. As cast members start the day, get into their job rotation, or greet the arriving guests, they all have this goal in mind—an attainable goal. Much like a 12,000-piece puzzle, everyone delivers a piece of the guest experience. Whether you load and unload the attractions, make the popcorn, dance on stage, keep the park clean, fix the light stand, rake the mulch, or perform in any part of the Parks and Resorts, you own and deliver a piece of the magic. And if a piece of the puzzle is missing, it becomes glaring. So cast members need to know that their performance matters and that everyone brings value. Every task contributes to the "big picture," and all the Disney cast members—or employees at your organization—collectively make the vision a reality. It is our job as leaders to connect the dots for them, articulate a compelling common purpose, and show them how significant their daily contribution is to the overarching vision. Some say being a leader is making people do what you want them to do. I disagree. I believe in commitment, not compliance. When employees know their roles and how they contribute to the final outcome, they are committed. They are more likely to do the right thing because they want to *and* they feel good about it.

Communicate your common purpose.

When I took over the Magic Kingdom, we were on the tail end of a massive expansion project that included doubling the size of Fantasyland and introducing a new fireworks show. The team had poured tons of energy and countless hours into meeting the deadlines of this new project. I felt the pixie dust had begun to lose its luster. It was time to reboot the common purpose for the organization and get cast members excited again. So I set upon reminding the team that we were first and foremost the "Most Magical Place on Earth" and that the Magic Kingdom is *the* place that gives Disney magic its name. It is the "first" park or the "only" park guests are going to visit (surely because no one else has such a castle!).

We had to make sure our common purpose of "We create magic!" permeated everything we did and all our interactions.

Instead of asking our employees, "How is your day going?" we would ask them, "What magic did you make happen today?" We made sure the Magic Kingdom's common purpose was in all forms of communication, such as internal publications, phone greetings ("Have a magical day!"), and backstage bulletin boards. It can be as simple as altering your organization's lingo to create constant reminders.

I also produced a weekly podcast of my team's priorities, which I sent to all the Magic Kingdom leaders, suggesting they share it with the entire cast. I chose my topics to convey what was a priority of mine and should become a priority of theirs.

I asked the entire leadership team to commit to being accessible and approachable in the operation and communicate why it was important to deliver magical memories. (Happy guests are loyal guests who return to the Magic Kingdom.) We all spent time in the park, role modeling; reinforcing the quality standards; and encouraging and recognizing the cast for making the guests feel special—all the while broadcasting our daily goal: "We are here to make the guests happy and to exceed all of their expectations."

During our daily briefings, we broadcasted "magical moments" or guest-letter comments. We recognized the cast members who had gone "above and beyond" and delivered the "magic touch" by singling out guests and finding ways to enhance their visit.

After several months, this produced the highest guest survey results in years. We celebrated our cast so that everyone could see and appreciate the immediate results of the team's hard work. Guests were telling us loud and clear that we were delivering on the "magic" factor.

A leader may be an incredible visionary, but without articulating the vision, convincingly selling it to the team, and role modeling it, employees can have a tough time aligning with the vision, buying into it, and ultimately delivering it. A clear vision must remain front and center, and we must be unwavering in communicating it.

Regularly reassess your vision.

Companies can easily become too immersed in running everyday business to think about the forecast. If we're lucky, the wind at our back pushes us in the right direction, but we sometimes have to face the unexpected headwinds of rapid changes. Competition is expanding with globalization; technology is transforming industries seemingly overnight; and climate change is affecting consumer behaviors with long-term impact. Big companies, because of their sheer size, bureaucracy, and red tape, often struggle to swiftly react to market trends and behavior changes, not to mention technological updates.

So we must take the time to assess our vision and strategic plan on a regular basis and make the necessary adjustments. History is littered with companies that have failed to tweak, recalibrate, or even revamp their visions, and most have gone bankrupt as a result (think of Kodak or Blockbuster). Too often, leaders hang on to a vision that has become unrealistic, outdated, or too far remote from the everyday business—by the time they realize this, it is either too late or too costly to change direction. As leaders, we must keep our eyes on the long game and must be bold about making required changes. Sometimes we have to change course, and sometimes we need the courage to change the destination entirely.

Fast Track to Results

Here are some key lessons on organizational vision:

- It is important for senior leadership to have a vision and to revisit it frequently for decision-making.
- Create a common purpose: a *modus operandi* to remember and one which employees at every level can contribute to on a daily basis.

- Reward, recognize, and tell stories about the ways employees in your organization are bringing the common purpose to life. This will encourage them to continue to perform these behaviors, and they will be role models for others to emulate.

Chapter 11
Strategy

In the Wild West days at Walt Disney World, any vice president could pitch any idea, and, if they were compelling enough with their idea, they would get the funding for a new project. It was not the most strategic way to make decisions, but it certainly taught people how to think creatively and tell a convincing story. Nowadays, Walt Disney World has become much more rigorous in building a strategy.

Every year we completed a study called the Needs Assessment. We evaluated each property, hotel, and park through filters such as marketing, sales, financial results, industrial engineering, food and beverage, retail, and most importantly, guest feedback. With each property's specific vision in mind, we examined how offerings measured up to guest expectations. If there were any gaps, we looked to alleviate the discrepancies with the relevant investments and capital projects. We could easily identify if we needed added capacity, new attractions, restaurants (table service or counter service), retail locations, shows, or simply additional bathroom facilities.

In the case of the Animal Kingdom, guests were telling us, for example, that it was a half-day destination without enough rides. So we decided to develop an additional land, Pandora, based on the movie *Avatar*, and add the Rivers of Lights night show to extend length of stay. At the Magic Kingdom, we needed a couple more table-service locations, so we opened the Skipper Canteen in Adventureland. With this process, we identified not only needs but also growth opportunities and positioning in relation to the rest of Walt Disney World. We could easily eliminate pet projects that did not pass the facts-and-logic test. All the departments built their individual strategy based on the same playbook, using the same format. The document would become the strategic guideline for the next five years. The Needs Assessment provided a consistent way to think about the overall business. As a result, we knew where we needed to focus our money and resources.

In 2011, I was the vice president of Disney's Hollywood Studios when I received a call from Walt Disney Imagineering (WDI). The team informed me that John Lassetter, Disney's chief creative officer and founder of Pixar, had an idea. And boy, was that a cool idea: Monsters, Inc. Door Coaster! In the movie's "scream factory" powering Monstropolis, doors move along a conveyor belt, providing monsters a portal to kids' bedrooms. John Lassetter envisioned a roller coaster taking the riders through the doors and into the bedrooms, much like the monsters. What a fun idea! This surely would be a popular attraction.

In most companies, when people receive this kind of call, they are all-in. If one of the big cheeses supports it, and the concept is compelling, what is there to discuss? Let's build it.

However, I knew the Hollywood Studios Needs Assessment inside and out, and the last thing we needed was another roller coaster. Because our strategy had been thoroughly vetted and based on sound analysis, I had the confidence to tactfully let them know that as much as we all loved the concept, the Studios did not need another coaster. "But, Dan, you heard him!" they said. "How cool would that attraction be in *your* park?" Yes, it would be very cool indeed, but the Assessment told a different story. At the time, the Studios had a total of two family attractions: the Great Movie Ride and Toy Story Midway Mania. Every other attraction in the park had either a height requirement (think Aerosmith Rock 'n' Roller Coaster, Twilight Zone Tower of Terror, and Star Tours) or was a stage show. If anything, we needed more family rides that appealed to the younger kids. The Needs Assessment tool eliminated pet projects and ensured we would not stray away from our ultimate goals.

Right or Left

Strategy stems from the vision you have created for your organization. In a way, it defines how your dreams will become reality. It creates a clear path to success and identifies each stepping stone to get you to this ambitious goal. This is the challenge we face as leaders: on the one hand, we have to be creative and envision the possibilities for our future, and on the other, we have to use rational thinking to build a strategy. Many leaders struggle with this because it ties together creative thinking (the right side of the brain) with logic (the left). We all have a dominant side guiding our thoughts and decisions. This probably explains why the most dynamic companies are often run by a duo of a visionary leader *and* a business-minded leader. Think Walt Disney and his brother Roy: Walt was the dreamer who would constantly look to the future with new ideas and innovations. Roy was the grounded leader, a bean-counter of sorts who would make sure the company did not go bankrupt in the process.

You instinctively know whether the left or right side of your brain most influences your thinking, and you can compensate by surrounding yourself with partners who bring the opposite approach. As you build your strategy, you must give a voice to partners who think differently. It is tempting to surround yourself with "yes" people to validate your own thinking, but creating a vision and building a sound strategy requires having complementary reasoning.

Strategy and Tactics

Strategy is a straightforward statement that defines your action plan for a department, while tactics are the result of sequential decisions. If our strategy was to bring an additional thrill ride to the Magic Kingdom, for example, the tactics would include identifying the intellectual property, the ride technology, the capacity needed, the location, and the required capital needed. Each would be in turn assigned to the appropriate department.

Inevitably, we would have to consider multiple options. Here is a simple tool that helped me assess the risk and compare each alternative. You can create and complete a grid like this when assessing risk in your organization. I used different colors (red, yellow, and green) to identify the impact of each option on our most important criteria. Red meant the option had a negative impact. Yellow meant the impact was neutral. Green meant the option made a positive impact. At the end, I gave an overall score, again using red, yellow, and green.

While the exercise is much more effective using colors, I use faces to make my point here because the book is not printed in color. In this case, smile = green, neutral = yellow, and frown = red.

RISK ASSESSMENT BY CATEGORY AND COLOR

Category	Customer	Employee	Financial	Operational	Public Relations	Overall
Option 1	🙂	☹️	😐	☹️	😐	☹️
Option 2	😐	🙂	🙂	😐	🙂	🙂
Option 3	😐	😐	🙂	🙂	☹️	😐

*You can add/subtract additional categories to rate risk.

This type of reasoning gave us an easy way to evaluate each option—and understand how each one compared in cost and impact on our public relations. Obviously, your criteria will differ depending on your activity. In the above example, Option 2 scored the highest with respect to its impact on our important criteria.

For the sake of consistency, I also found it relevant to integrate the different options with our quality standards to see if each individual alternative would advance Safety, Courtesy, Show, and Efficiency (more on these standards in the next chapter).

RISK ASSESSMENT BY CATEGORY AND COLOR

Category	Safety	Courtesy	Show	Efficiency	Overall
Option 1	☺	☹	😐	☹	☹
Option 2	😐	☺	☺	😐	☺
Option 3	😐	😐	☺	☺	😐

This provided me with a quick snapshot and created a clear path for the decision-making process. In this example, Option 2 was the clear choice, as it scored highest with respect to both the impact on each important criteria and the advancement of our quality standards.

Admittedly, I never made a decision on my own. I relied heavily on my team and encouraged them to be critical and challenge my thinking. When discussing our strategy, I always wanted someone to be the devil's advocate and bring up all the obstacles and flaws of our action plan. You can purposely assign that role to someone at the table and have them raise any and every objection. When you give permission to make critical comments, you and your team can effectively prevent pitfalls and anticipate roadblocks.

Fᴀsᴛ Tʀᴀᴄᴋ ᴛᴏ Rᴇsᴜʟᴛs

Build a strategic plan:

- Take time to step away from the daily grind of running your business and think about the mid-term and long-term needs through the filters of financial, employee, and customer needs.

- Use a Needs Assessment method, a Strengths, Weaknesses, Opportunities, and Threats (SWOT) analysis, or other tool to evaluate your organization and help determine needs.

- Include as many departments as possible to contribute to your strategic plan.

- Give permission to critique the project (or initiative) in order to uncover challenges.

- Update your plan annually, and refer to it often when considering new projects to ensure alignment.

Chapter 12

Quality Standards

The Lopez family is on a long-awaited vacation to Walt Disney World. It's the trip of a lifetime for this multigenerational family of six: Mom, Dad, the three kids, and 79-year-old Grandma. The kids are happily bouncing around as Mom and Dad take turns pushing Grandma, who uses a wheelchair. She is able-bodied but has poor balance and tires easily.

They approach Spaceship Earth at Epcot and park the wheelchair in the designated space. Grandma walks the few yards to approach the loading zone. This area consists of a moving walkway that matches the speed of Spaceship Earth's traveling vehicles, thus allowing the rider to board safely. The cast member in charge of loading, Katie, quickly assesses Grandma's mobility. The loading process requires a bit of coordination, and there is a slight risk that Grandma may lose her balance. What to do?

Katie immediately brings the ride to a complete stop so that Grandma can board safely. This decision will undoubtedly increase the wait time for eager riders who have been standing patiently in line. The guests currently aboard Spaceship Earth, meanwhile, will have their time-travel experience temporarily interrupted and will be "brought back to Earth" by a safety message asking them to "remain seated until travel can resume."

Yet despite the slowed-down loading process, the increased wait time, and the show's disruption, the cast member did not hesitate to make this swift decision. Why? Because she was trained to operate within a precise framework allowing her to make impromptu decisions. At all times, a clear set of rules guided her judgment: the Disney quality standards of **Safety, Courtesy, Show, Efficiency**.

In this particular case, Katie realized that something may have to be compromised to ensure safety. But her training and the *priority ranking* of the quality standards prepared her for this very situation.

Have quality standards or bust!

Disney leaders carefully selected the quality standards, or Four Keys, of the company's success from what visitors expected from the organization. If you were to survey guests about why they chose Disney, the vast majority would rank "Courtesy" as their deciding factor. They love the smiling and friendly cast members as well as the cleanliness of the place. In addition, guests rave about the shows, fireworks, and attention to details, and they always enjoy the seamless experience and easy processes. As for Safety, guests seldom mention it as it is considered a "given." However, the Disney organization chose to make Safety a quality standard because of the sheer volume of visitors and the complexity of theme park operations. Besides, none of the delights of vacationing at Walt Disney World would be possible if safety were compromised in any way!

Based on these findings, Disney level of service aims to provide all four standards—Safety, Courtesy, Show, and Efficiency—at every interaction. When the time comes to pick a vacation destination, guests can reliably expect these four quality standards. It makes their choice simple and easy.

The upside for leaders is also simple: when frontline employees such as Katie are fully prepared to make spur-of-the-moment decisions and address every possible scenario, leaders can delegate the decision-making process and run a more efficient and reliable operation.

Rank your standards in order of priority.

Similar stories to the Lopez family's play out many times each day at Walt Disney World. If you have been to a character meet-and-greet, you have probably noticed that the line can be pretty long. When your kids finally get to meet Mickey in person, a Disney photographer is on hand to capture the magical moment, which you can purchase online for $15.99. However, you can also use your own camera, and cast members will often offer to take the picture themselves so you can be included in the shot. Why? Because Courtesy *supersedes* Efficiency in the list of standards, even when it delays the entire process and reduces Disney's bottom line. Courtesy is a commitment Disney has made to its guests wherever and whenever possible. It is what builds guest loyalty and is a decision factor when the time comes to book a vacation. Even if they don't know Disney's quality standards, guests specifically remember how they felt when a cast member sacrificed Efficiency (and profitability) in favor of Courtesy, and in the long run, this investment pays big dividends.

The company carefully selected and classified these quality standards *in order of priority* to facilitate the decision-making process. All cast members know them and when prompted, will list them in order of importance: Safety, Courtesy, Show, and Efficiency.

It's all about behaviors!

Going back to the Lopez family situation: Katie, the cast member, knew right away what had to come first. The awaiting guests probably flinched at the delay and gave the cast member a collective sigh of irritation. Likewise, the riders experienced an interrupted show, but, if an accident were to have happened with Grandma, the consequences would have been far worse. The cast member did not need to call a leader or ask her peers. On day one of her training, Katie learned the importance of the Four Keys as essential for every guest's interaction.

Which brings me to my next point: having quality standards is vital for the success of any organization, but it will make a difference only if the supporting behaviors are plainly and clearly defined—for three main reasons.

First, it would be pointless to tell employees to demonstrate quality standards if these behaviors were left to their interpretation. Who knows, for example, where their personal "Safety" threshold is? What do they deem a "Courteous" demeanor? What is their interpretation of "Show?" And they may lack perspective to assess what is "Efficient." So it is up to the leader and the organization to be clear and lay out the details of what is appropriate or not.

Second, quality standards translate differently from one department to another. In a retail shop, Safety may require employees to bend their knees when doing heavy lifting, or to avoid a water sprinkler when storing boxes. In Food and Beverage, frequent hand washing is essential to maintain food sanitation requirements. In the Human Resources department, Safety implies that all employee information is kept confidential. In the IT department, we want to make sure that the organization's system cannot be hacked—and so on.

Last but not least, communicating specific behavior expectations is essential in today's diverse workforce. During my career, I have learned that different cultures can have pretty contrasting interpretations when it comes to service behaviors. As vice president of Epcot, I had the singular (yet greatly rewarding) responsibility of managing the World Showcase of eleven different countries. Not only did I have to be mindful of each nationality's sensibility but also understand its unique-ness. For instance, Japanese cast members will never directly say "no" to a request and may engage in lengthy alternative propositions that can baffle an American customer. Japanese team members have a deep sense of hospitality and deliver outstanding customer service. However, addressing one-of a-kind situations and providing impromptu custom-ized service may be more challenging if they don't have clear guidelines. Chinese employees have a different tolerance for interpersonal space and tend to stand very close to people in public places. Meanwhile, cast members from Latin cultures (Mexicans, Italians) are very demonstra-tive and are inclined to make physical contact in communicating their care and affection. Some Americans think of French waiters and wait-resses as being either aloof or disrespectful because of how direct they are. (An unusual request may be promptly met with a quick "C'est pas possible!"). A French waiter has been trained to be efficient and discreet, to never interrupt a dinner, and more importantly, to never bring the check unless it has been requested.

Any of the above behaviors may fall out of the realm of what Ameri-cans consider courteous. While appropriate in their respective countries, I found such behaviors did not align with the understanding and expec-tations of the American clientele, not to mention the Disney approach to service. With this in mind, it became imperative that we define the specific behaviors that supported the quality standards we had put in place. We made sure these detailed behaviors were imparted to the cast members during their training.

The critical ingredient to successfully selecting and implementing quality standards lies in the details. First, understand exactly what cus-tomers expect; then rank quality standards in order of priority to allow for quick decision-making; finally, provide the precise behaviors expected from your frontline employees through extensive training, recognition, and coaching.

Fast Track to Results

These are key lessons on quality standards:

- Create quality standards that make sense for your organization and reflect the expectations of your customers or guests. They should be relevant and prioritized in order of importance.
- Once your quality standards are established, look at each role in your organization, and determine the specific behaviors that are required to deliver them.
- Make sure your quality standards permeate all the decision making throughout your organization.
- Incorporate your quality standards and ensuing behaviors into your training program as well as all forms of recognition and performance evaluation.

Chapter 13

Training

I n 2006, I finished my six-year run in the hotel side of Walt Disney World and made my way back to the theme parks, specifically, as General Manager of Magic Kingdom Merchandise. I went to my "tried and true" playbook for taking a new job, and started training in every area of the Merchandise operation. My goal was to be able to walk into the Emporium—the Main Street USA shop responsible for 25% of Magic Kingdom merchandise sales—and be able to jump on a register to help out during busy times.

During training, I immersed myself in the retail business: where to find merchandise, how to process a refund or exchange, how to close the register at the end of the day ... I learned the different retail locations and met cast members and leaders from all Merchandise areas of the park. I identified both our strengths and opportunities for improvement along the way. I was also able to evaluate the training process of new Merchandise cast members. Nothing is more valuable and revealing than getting firsthand experience!

At the end, I completed a survey on my training experience, as all new cast members do.

Fast forward six months. We were struggling with our Merchandise guest-satisfaction scores. I read through the survey answers and tried to find where we were falling short. One particular rating caught my attention: "Was the cast member you interacted with friendly and helpful?" The score was lower than I thought it should be.

I regularly walked the operation and observed our employees doing a pretty good job greeting guests as they entered the shops. The cast members smiled, paid attention to kids, and were generally attentive. I thought back to my own training and felt good about the way my trainer had role-modeled the expectations: he was friendly to the guests and engaged whenever possible. So what were we missing? In search of an answer, I went to talk to Kalissa, one of our superstar Merchandise leaders and an excellent thought partner. I shared my findings with her and asked for input. Obviously, Kalissa had been thinking about it also. "Dan, do you think that friendly and helpful are the same thing?" I knew right away she was onto something.

Design your training based on the experience your customer expects.

Too often, we build training programs that are exclusively based on what the operation requires: how to run a register, cook food, drive a vehicle, or clean a room—and promptly forget the outcome. In the situation above, we were focusing heavily on creating the right interaction between the employee and the guests but not necessarily preparing our cast members to help find the item customers wanted to buy. So we were training our cast members to deliver Courtesy, but we omitted training for Efficiency. Cast members did not know where to find out-of-stock products or how to suggest alternative options, and they were frustrating guests in the process.

As we dug into the issue, we realized our guests agreed we were "friendly" but did not consider our cast members "helpful"—hence the poor rating. The training failed to match the guest expectations for service. We also realized we lacked the right tools for the cast members to deliver that service in the first place. Clearly, our training program was missing a key component of what our guests expected. Ultimately, we closed the gap and equipped our cast members with iPads so they could track products around the property and help guests find their coveted souvenirs.

This experience gave me a deep understanding of the requirements of a successful training program: when done right, it should equip the trainees with all the tools necessary to deliver the service *based on the customers' expectations*. As for conducting guest surveys, we need to ask pointed questions to get realistic and holistic feedback.

Design comprehensive training.

When we overly focus training on the technical part of the job, the trainee tends to forget about what he or she is supposed to achieve. At Disney, this goal was to create magic.

An effective way to build a great training program is to deliver the information through the filter of our common purpose and quality standards. For example, before handling food, Food and Beverage employees must wash their hands for as long as it takes to sing "Happy Birthday." If I were the trainer, I would wash my hands, then have the trainees wash theirs to ensure technical knowledge, and then remind them about the Safety key, which should impress upon them the importance of handwashing.

At Disneyland Paris, the team training cast members to drive the vehicles on Main Street had a great approach. The first day of training was focused solely on the cast members' roles as citizens of Main Street—how to interact with guests (as part of our Courtesy standard); how to create games and magical moments for children; the history of Main Street, and the specifics of the antique cars they were driving (as part of our Show element). In other words, they learned the full history of the scene in which they would be playing a role. The next two days were focused on the technical and procedural side of actually loading, unloading, and driving the vehicles (as part of our Safety and Efficiency standards). The design of the training on day one emphasized the importance of entertaining guests—their *common purpose* while the training on day two and three emphasized how to actually operate the vehicles—their *role*.

With technical skills, precision matters.

Sending untrained employees to perform is unfair, will damage their confidence in the early days of their employment, and could put your organization at risk. When I spoke to new employees during roundtable discussions, I would often hear of a discrepancy between the training they had just received and what the operation actually practiced.

There were two possible reasons for this: either the training guide was out of date and irrelevant (manuals were not always updated in a timely way); or the trainer did not believe that the documented procedure was the best or most efficient way to get the job done and would train "their own way." This can have dire consequences.

Take the "lock-out/tag" process as an example. Whenever Engineering was working on equipment, they were required to lock out the circuit breaker with a physical padlock. This was meant to prevent activation of the breaker during maintenance work, which could cause electrocution. Let's imagine that because "locking out" adds extra time to the job, and since nobody has ever been electrocuted, it now has become common practice to just tape a note on the breaker instead. New hires, always quick to emulate more senior employees, start adopting the same approach. Then one day, the note falls off, someone flips the breaker and triggers the power, not knowing that someone else is working on the line. This is an extreme example with extreme consequences, but this is how safety measures gradually deteriorate. As a leader, you need to make sure your trainers and the operation employees understand that there is only *one way to perform* any procedure. If something can be improved or done more efficiently, fine—submit it for approval and change the documentation to do it differently. But the takeaway here is that you must insist on absolute consistency between the training process and what is practiced in the operation.

"The only thing worse than training employees and losing them is not to train them and keep them."
—Zig Ziglar

Assess for competency.

The end stage of any training must confirm the trainee has fully *learned* and understood all the necessary information and, most importantly, that the trainee is *capable of performing* the various tasks. Someone independent from the trainer—preferably a leader—must perform this assessment.

At Disney, we called these KAPAs (Knowledge Assessments and Performance Assessments). At the end of training, the trainer would schedule time for the trainee and frontline leader to sit down and discuss the training.

The leader would first pepper the trainee with questions from the training manual.

For example:

- "Tell me how to perform a refund."
- "If you see a guest or fellow cast member lying on the ground, what do you do?"
- "If you hear a strange noise while dispatching trains on your attraction, what do you do?"
- "What is the greeting for this location?"
- "What do you do if you find a lost child?"

- "Name the allergens that we need to be aware of in Food and Beverage."

As you can see, some of the questions were specific to the role the cast member was going to perform, and others were procedures for all employees in the park, regardless of work assignment.

Then, the cast member would go through a performance assessment. They were required to demonstrate they had learned the relevant processes (ie. how to perform a refund). The leader would observe them working for a short period of time to confirm that they understood how to perform their role. It was a good time for the leader to provide additional feedback if needed.

Sometimes the result of the knowledge/performance assessment would result in another day of training, or, in rare cases, moving the cast member to another role. In most instances, the leader would sign off the cast member as ready to perform independently. The newly trained cast member would also sign off on the completion of their training. This formalized the process and helped the new cast member understand the importance of their role.

In any organization, all employees should be regularly reevaluated on the behaviors and processes learned in training. This may seem like a logical step but too often a neglected one. Much like in the breaker example, I found multiple discrepancies that gradually appeared between what had been imparted during training and the common practice in the operation.

Over time, we all acquire bad habits. Think about how often you forget to put on your turn signal when driving. You were trained to use it but become complacent and eventually negligent. It is the same in businesses. Often, seasoned employees have developed bad habits that they role model. Before you know it, new trainees start emulating them.

Whatever evaluation process you use (leader audits, assessments, or secret shopper programs, to name a few), it must examine the behaviors and evaluate them against the training that is provided.

Fast Track to Results

The best training programs are developed with the following considerations:

- Training is an investment, not a cost. Make sure it is detailed and thorough.
- Training needs to be based on the technical requirements of the role as well as the quality standards and corresponding behaviors.
- Training must be aligned throughout the process; from standard operating guidelines and training material to training delivery and assessment. If your company changes a procedure or standard, all parts of the process must reflect that change.

Chapter 14

Development

As I prepared to leave Disney in March 2018, the company already had about a half dozen candidates for the job, thanks to its great development program and constant preparation for the future. The company soon named Jason Kirk, originally an industrial engineer who had plenty of park experience as a general manager, as my deserving successor. At the time, Jason was the vice president of Transportation for Walt Disney World, and he had expressed interest in moving to a park VP role. This enabled a quick selection, and Jason and I were able to work together to transition before I departed. Such an effective development process requires discipline and forward thinking to maintain.

The Long Game

Development differs from training. While training imparts skills that immediately benefit the organization, development allows the individual to grow over a long period of time.

Much like in a garden, you plant a seed; you fertilize that seed by providing development opportunities in the form of coaching, mentoring, and job rotation; and you let it bloom. In order to keep people happy, fulfilled, and engaged, leaders need to give their team members an opportunity to expand their knowledge and further their careers. Ultimately, developing people will ensure the well-being of your organization. As opportunities arise, you should have a pool of employees who are ready to step up because you have cultivated their potential.

Our goal at Disney was to have a list of successors for each executive and senior-level position in the organization—not an easy task. We kept this list updated so that when someone left or was promoted, we could look at the list and consider those candidates to ensure a quick transition. In the meantime, we'd prepare potential successors with new experiences, classes, and other enriching opportunities.

Emerging Leaders

To fill higher-level roles at Disney, we also identified and informed promising candidates, who would enter the "Emerging Leaders" pool. We constantly gave them opportunities to expand their knowledge throughout the organization, for months or even years. My advice to young, up-and-coming leaders was always the same: Be curious, learn, learn, learn, and remember it is not only about who you know but mainly about who knows you—so get as much exposure as possible. Meet people, network, volunteer for new assignments, and challenge yourself by going out of your comfort zone. Once we formalized the leadership-selection process, we required candidates to attend certain classes to prepare for the roles.

I got great satisfaction in seeing leaders who had started at an entry level in one of my teams move up through the organization. I always considered developing leaders a priority and hoped that it was a reflection of my leadership style. I also knew full well that if my high-performing direct reports were not given a chance to move up, they would move out. Besides, I was just returning the favor extended to me during my twenty-six years from my starting role as a parking attendant at Epcot and through the nineteen different positions that ensued.

Development as a Performance Goal

Development was an ongoing process at Disney and permeated all levels of the organization. Each leader had to establish his or her own development path, which Disney would formalize as part of the annual performance evaluation. So a leader would be rated not only on performance (business results and leadership behaviors) but also on personal development accomplishments. When conducting annual evaluations with my direct reports, I made sure they had a development plan. I wanted to know their career aspirations, learning needs, and interests to help them prepare for future roles. Beyond that, the onus was on them to develop themselves. Though not everyone will be promoted to roles with larger scope and responsibility, it should not exclude anyone from having a development plan. As a leader, you should always encourage people to learn and get better, regardless of future aspirations.

Companies often neglect—or even skip completely—the development process because it does not fill an immediate need. However, when high-performing employees see no path for their future, they will go and find their happiness somewhere else.

A good development program allows organizations to be more nimble and reduces the time needed to get qualified candidates into new roles. It also reduces turnover, and a more experienced workforce is more productive, thus reducing the recruitment and training costs.

Fast Track to Results

Integrate development into your organization:

- Make sure everyone in your organization regardless of level or potential has a development plan. Assessing personal development should be a part of the performance evaluation.
- Agree on the development plan through collaborative effort with the direct report. However, it needs to be formulated and driven mostly *by the direct report.*
- The development plan should reflect competencies the direct report will need for future roles, as well as competencies the organization will require.

Chapter 15

Measurement

Measurement is a tricky business. Often the easy things to measure don't matter, and we can't easily measure the most important things. Our measurements might encourage unintended behaviors. At times, we implement such a plethora of comprehensive measurements that we create a dynamic of "When everything is important, nothing is important." Here, we will explore cases where measurement has worked and other times failed miserably.

Unintended Consequences

In the late '90s, Disney decided to more proactively reduce Food & Beverage waste, partially by tying the executive chefs' bonus to their cost of sales. All eyes were on this particular metric, which resulted in some unintended consequences. To earn their bonus, chefs cut cost by using lesser-quality products, streamlining menus, and duplicating ingredients among various recipes. They got the savings indeed, but the guest-satisfaction surveys took a serious hit. By putting too much weight on this particular measurement, we inadvertently caused the food quality and revenue to drop.

Lagging vs. Leading Indicators

Too often, we put emphasis on the wrong metrics. Let's use Safety, the most important quality standard at Walt Disney World, as an example. Most companies use the OSHA (Occupational Safety and Health Administration) rate, which measures the number of accidents requiring more than first aid as a percentage of total hours worked, as well as lost time percentage, days away from work, and workers' comp, among other factors. However, focusing on these metrics—which are all important to track and understand—does not improve the outcome because they are lagging indicators and report only what happened in the past. To improve safety, we must move farther upstream and examine the behaviors and culture that might be causing accidents. What we found at Disney was that by measuring culture, we could start measuring how proactive we were in terms of safety *before* accidents occurred.

We first looked at how executives and managers demonstrated a Safety commitment. If, as the vice president of the Magic Kingdom, I did not talk about safety, include safety items on my meeting agendas, do safety walks, and react quickly to feedback about unsafe conditions, I could not expect my team to prioritize Safety.

As I've mentioned, role modeling is the most powerful form of communicating priorities. So, during performance reviews and touch-bases with my direct reports, I asked each general manager about safety initiatives for each area of responsibility. If they had a clearly developed communication plan and they understood the key areas of risk in their department, I could be fairly sure that their accident rates would be lower than the average.

Consistent monthly safety meetings with frontline cast members were another important measurement. We could capture and follow up on the issues bubbling up in these meetings, and later communicate the results back to the employees.

The last measurement was "near miss" reporting. Often the difference between an accident and a near miss is just luck and timing. In order to strengthen the Disney Safety culture, we trained our teams to treat a near miss just like an accident, with the same sense of urgency. For example, if a cast member slipped in the kitchen and kept his balance without any injury, we would still ask him to fill out a near miss accident report. What were the conditions when he almost fell? Was the floor wet? Was he running because he was in a hurry? We would submit these near misses for review by the local safety committee each month. Then, the team would improve the conditions to avoid future accidents—in this case, fix a chip in the floor or add a checklist item to dry the floors more frequently.

Here is another best practice to adopt.

One day, Walt Disney World executives asked senior leaders to join a conference call about an urgent issue. The vice president of Safety announced that guests just had been killed on a flume ride in an Australian theme park. I was confused for a few minutes. I was pretty sure we did not have a Disney park in Australia. *Why were we talking about this?* The call proceeded to address possible causes of the accident on this particular ride. The next question was whether we operated any flume rides at any Disney theme parks manufactured by the same company, and whether we had any risk of any of our flume rides capsizing. Now *this* is a sign of a world-class safety culture! An incident happens on the other side of the world in a competitor's theme park, and instead of being glad that it was not us, we get on a call to determine if this could happen to us. A near miss indeed!

So, if you want to improve your performance, be sure to focus on the lagging indicators (outcomes), *and* the leading indicators that impact the behaviors.

Real Time

Another one of the top criteria of effective measurement is the importance of operating in real time. As mentioned above, if we constantly focus on lagging indicators of performance, we will fall behind and miss our opportunity to correct the problems.

At Disney, we were avid users of the Net Promoter Score (NPS), a great tool to collect immediate feedback on our operation and the quality of service we had delivered. (I encourage you to Google NPS to learn more about the process.) The NPS allowed us to get timely feedback on our locations, identify great and poor performers in our operation, and immediately either recognize or coach them.

Real-time measuring tools were a priority for Disney, and remain so.

For instance, Walt Disney World bus transportation is an important part of the overall experience as resort guests travel between our hotels and our parks. While the transportation team does an excellent job of transporting tens of thousands of guests safely and efficiently every day, there are moments when they miss their service standard goals.

In the past, if a bus was late due to traffic or an accident, the guests would wait significantly longer to get to the parks, and might write a complaint letter about how they missed their meal, show, FastPass window, fireworks, or meet-and-greet with a favorite character. At that point, our only option was to provide a refund, free tickets, or discount on a future visit. As we rolled out My Magic Plus, however, we could begin to leverage the technology in the bands, which serve as room keys, credit cards, tickets, and FastPasses.

Enter real-time data. Today, when a guest bound for the Magic Kingdom arrives at the bus stop, a sensor detects the Magic Band RFID in the zone, and a timer starts. If that particular Magic Band has not boarded a bus within a certain period of time, we can assume that the bus was late. That data is instantly paged to the Magic Kingdom Transportation manager, who can now have his team meet the bus upon arrival, apologize for the extended wait, and correct the situation right on the spot by providing FastPasses to make up for lost time.

Not every organization has this kind of technology at its disposal, but there are some simpler ways to get real-time measurements. For example, each GM of the various Disney resorts delivers an in-room letter to all guests with his or her personal phone number or a link and QR code directing them to a website that helps them report any issues they encounter. The number or website immediately connects their call or message to the duty manager, who can immediately correct the situation on behalf of the general manager. Subsequently, the issue goes through a root-cause analysis so the resort can swiftly fix the process breakdown *(see example on next page)*.

"We cannot improve what we cannot measure."

Through the Lens of Your Quality Standards

In any organization, consistency brings credibility and efficiency. As discussed earlier, all your team members should operate within the same framework—one common purpose and clear quality standards. Ideally, you will have selected these quality standards based on your customer or guest expectations. With the same reasoning, you should have a training program emphasizing the behaviors that support these quality standards. The next logical step is measuring performance through the quality-standard lens.

At Disney, we would always measure all four quality standards: Safety (as described above), Courtesy, Show, and Efficiency. The NPS as well as secret shopper programs gave us a good read on our Courtesy metrics:

Thank you for being our Guest!

My name is Kelly Kline, General Manager of Disney's All-Star Sports Resort, and my team and I are here to help fill your stay with Disney magic! We want to ensure that you have a memorable vacation in the heart of the *Walt Disney World*™ Resort.

As you enjoy your stay, our Cast Members will strive to provide you with extraordinary service. If you happen to experience something that was not quite right during your visit, please let me know. Ensuring an enjoyable vacation for all of our Guests is of the utmost importance to us. On the other hand, if something during your trip thoroughly delights you or if one of our Cast Members makes a special impression, I'd love to hear about it. We take great pride in thanking our Cast Members for a job well done.

If you would like to share thoughts about your stay, please contact me through this tool *diz.sv/sportstay* or use the QR code below. Please allow us the opportunity to address your comments while you are still on property.

I look forward to hearing from you and wish you the most magical stay at Disney's All-Star Sports Resort.

Warmest regards,

Kelly Kline,
General Manager
Disney's All-Star Sports Resort

- Were you greeted when you walked in?
- Was the cast member readily available?
- Was he/she smiling?
- Did he/she make eye contact?

We measured our Show standard with pointed leader audits:

- Was the cast member wearing a name tag?
- Was their appearance in accordance to Disney grooming guidelines?
- Was the area clean and free of debris?

The Maintenance department would inspect paint, concrete, and lights on a regular basis while Custodial leaders would always inspect bathrooms and areas for cleanliness—all important Show elements.

As for Efficiency, we could compare data from retail, restaurants, and attractions, to name a few, in measuring performance against the quality standard.

These may seem like a given, but too often we generate measurements misaligned with the desired outcome. The bigger the organization, the more "reports" we seem to produce. Beware of overmeasuring. Stick to the basic, most significant metrics and, more importantly, follow through on the data. It is better to have few metrics that you read and address methodically than be buried under a pile of data that nobody acts upon.

Fast Track to Results

For effective measurement:

- It should happen in real time, and use leading indicators whenever possible.
- Just because you can measure something does not mean that you should measure it. Measure only relevant and important things.
- Have as few measures as possible enabling you to monitor your organization effectively. Extract the learnings and take action.

Chapter 16

Accessibility and Approachability

A leader can create great communication with one simple act: becoming accessible and approachable to everyone in the organization. When I realized the value of relationship-building, this became my daily goal. And I always remembered that it may be intimidating for a frontline employee or entry-level leader to interact with an executive, so I approached everyone with humility.

Like many Disney executives, I created a confidential voicemail number and plastered it all over the Magic Kingdom: on bulletin boards, in break rooms, in the cafeteria. I wanted all 12,000 cast members to know who I was and that I was available to speak to them. Now, I had to set some clear expectations. My goal was *not* for every cast member to call me on every issue or idea they had, so the notices included my voicemail number and read something like this:

"Hi, my name is Dan Cockerell, and I am the vice president of the Magic Kingdom. If at any time you feel like you need to bring an issue to me, I am available on my confidential voicemail. Please leave a message, and if you would like me to call you back, leave your name and phone number. We have an excellent leadership team, and if you have any ideas, problems, or questions, I strongly suggest that you reach out to your direct leader first. But I am always available if you feel you need to talk to me directly. Thank you for creating magic!"

When people called the voicemail number, they would also be instructed to call me on my personal phone number in case it was really urgent. People thought I was crazy to allow this kind of access. However, in a big place such as Disney, communication does not always flow well or fast, and I wanted to make sure that I had an opportunity to be aware of an issue, instead of finding out through Facebook, Instagram, *The Orlando Sentinel*, the State Sanitation Department, Channel Nine News, or worse, my boss.

The messages I received ranged from suggestions on how to improve the guest experience and safety issues to thank-yous and "You gotta be kidding me" messages. Others were about bureaucratic dysfunctionality in pay and other administrative processes, and still others were about interpersonal conflicts the cast member was having with peers or leadership.

This approach had two pitfalls. The first is what I called the "frequent flyers." Some cast members decided they were going to call me for every wrong they felt had ever been done to them. Or, they would raise issues that clearly could be addressed locally, but instead they liked the idea of informing the VP of the park. After a string of such calls, I would meet with the cast member in question, thank them for reaching out to me, and retrain them on how to elevate issues—mainly, by always giving their leaders an opportunity to respond to them first.

The second pitfall was the potential trust I could lose from my direct reports by seemingly overreaching and micromanaging conflict situations. The danger was in listening to a story from a cast member, taking what they told me at 100% face value, and peppering the GM of the department involved, thus questioning their ability to deal with issues.

I was familiar with a certain conflict dynamic from my kids when they were little. Jullian would annoy his sister, Margot, to the point that he could elicit a reaction. She would hit him, and he would report to us from the back seat that she had hit him for no reason. Then, in the injustice of all injustices, Margot would get in trouble for hitting her brother. What we learned as we raised our kids was that during a conflict, there are facts and perceptions, and the fault is seldom with one person.

This played out with some of the calls I would get from cast members. Some told me that their leaders were showing favoritism, and unfortunately, they were not the favored one! Others would tell me that they thought their leaders were targeting them and holding them to a higher accountability level than their team members.

I quickly sensed that my being involved in such matters could be an issue with my direct reports, so I prepared my team in advance. Here is a summary of my message to them:

> *We have 12,000 cast members. If you think that we are not always going to have conflicts, disagreements, and discord among our cast, then you are living in Fantasyland!*
>
> *I would much rather have our cast talk to us instead of others about their issues. I see it as a great opportunity for us to build trust through our willingness to listen and act.*
>
> *Just because someone calls me does not mean that they are right. However, it does mean that they have a concern. I will listen to their problems and make it clear that I need to get the whole story before rendering a point of view.*

I am part of this leadership team, and I am ultimately accountable for all the cast experience. As such, I consider myself an additional set of eyes and ears to help make us all successful.

If a cast member left a message and remained anonymous, I would, with no judgment, forward the voicemail to the appropriate leader who could explore if there was indeed an issue or a valuable suggestion to be implemented. If the message was part of a trend, I would ask the GM to research the underpinnings.

If a cast member left a message with a name and number, I would call back personally and discuss the issue in depth. I would always ask if they had already elevated the issue to their direct leaders. If they had not, I would help them find ways to address it at that level.

No matter what the issue, whether I agreed or not, I would always thank the person for reaching out and encourage them to continue to speak up. In meetings and in my communication with the park employees, I would make sure to reference the valuable calls I had received to encourage others to speak up.

By including this level of approachability, we were able to hear many more voices and dig beneath the surface of what was going on in the park. Also, because I was role modeling my willingness to be accessible to everyone, the rest of the leadership team started emulating those behaviors—some to become better leaders and some, I suspect, out of self-preservation. If they did not listen and resolve issues, there was a good chance the cast member was going to elevate it to the next level or eventually to me.

"Power creates distance. Leaders bridge the gap."
—Phil Wilson

Do not leave communication to chance.

While working in the various Disney resorts and theme parks, I realized that the best ideas, the right concerns, and the most passionate pleas do not always make it up the chain of command. I also learned that if issues are not addressed internally, to leadership, they can easily be shared externally, to everyone! (Think Facebook, Twitter, local newspapers, and local television stations.)

It's not frequent for internal organizational issues to boil over and get outside the company, but when it happens, it is a threat to the brand.

During my time at Disney, I also learned how important it was for everyone to have a voice. How frustrating is it when you have an idea, or want to improve something, or want to fix something and nobody listens? Very frustrating!

So, I made it my goal to be someone who is approachable and accessible. Every day, this goal was on my mind, from where I showed up to where I ate lunch, to my demeanor when walking around the park. Everything I did signaled, "I am excited to be here and want to hear your thoughts!"

Being approachable and accessible as a leader has many advantages and some disadvantages. The good greatly outweighs the bad!

Let's start with the disadvantages. First, you have to be "on" most of the time. Everything we project verbally and nonverbally has to be inviting. Let's call it curb appeal. Employees are already a little wary about talking to you, just because of your title. To project servant leadership, your message has to be that the employees and their concerns are more important than anything the leaders are doing. That statement has the benefit of being true. They perform better, we get better results, and we are held accountable to the results we get!

Being "on" takes a lot of energy, self-awareness, and intent. We cannot afford to have bad days or moments of unfriendliness. That is how reputations are damaged or destroyed.

The second disadvantage is that we receive a lot of calls, emails, and texts. Often, our first reaction is to direct them to their manager, and that may very well be the final solution, but we need to have the patience to listen to their issue or idea in a respectful way.

The last disadvantage is the risk of being perceived as the sole problem-solver for the organization. If someone calls us and we solve their issue, then we end up circumventing the management team and potentially create a gap in their credibility with the employee. All leaders get pretty nervous when their employees are talking to people a few rungs up the organizational ladder.

On the plus side, you get to hear the truth faster, which enables you to react immediately and correct course if needed. I call this a bureaucracy buster. Moreover, you set an example that can be emulated at other levels of the organization. But the reality is that we have here a dilemma! There is no straight answer. How do we work through the organizational chart to get work done, and at times ignore that chart to talk to everyone and anyone in our companies? Not easy, but boy, when we do it right, it's extremely effective in making improvements in our employee and customer experience.

Fast Track to Results

Consider these key insights on accessibility and approachability:

- If you have an assistant, talk to him or her about going from stern gatekeeper to friendly greeter.
- Schedule time on your calendar to walk around and talk to employees in your organization. Make sure you are welcoming input.
- Dine frequently in your local cafeteria with your employees.
- Give people your phone number and email, and encourage them to reach out to you.
- Always thank people for contacting you whether you can help them or not.

Chapter 17

Partnering and Collaborating

In late 2017, I came across a video of one of the Amazon fulfillment centers. As you can imagine, these warehouses are highly efficient and employ a variety of robots and box-shuffling people to fill the millions of orders put in every day. The warehouse floor contains tiny QR codes to help the robots move about the rows and pick the appropriate items off the shelves.

Seeing the video gave me an idea. As VP of the Magic Kingdom, I was responsible for what went on not only *in* the park, but also *under* the park. I am referring to the fabled Magic Kingdom tunnel or, as we called it internally, the Utilidor. At Disney, we used this underground tunnel, which stretches to all the different lands of the park, to transport supplies to Food & Beverage, Merchandise, and other locations without interfering with the magic. The Utilidor also contains cast cafeterias, wardrobe, and locker rooms, among other behind-the-scenes departments.

Obviously, the Utilidor sees a lot of activity, so we always looked for opportunities to improve the traffic flow. We were also constantly struggling with the number of pallets left in the Utilidor as they presented a fire code safety hazard. That's why the Amazon video had piqued my curiosity. *What if we had robots move the empty pallets back to the entrance of the tunnel, thus solving our safety issue? It could even morph into a complete automatization of all the pallet delivery to and from the main entrance of the Utilidor!* The idea was intriguing but, honestly, I had no clue if it had any merit or even how to get started. It all seemed very complex but, as they say, "There is an island of opportunity in the middle of every difficulty." So I went in search of help.

During my years at Disney, I had worked jointly on a variety of initiatives with Ron Mills, who was by then the VP of Distribution Services—just the perfect thought partner I needed. He immediately saw the potential, agreed to conduct a study of the project, and assigned one of his team members to the initiative. Then, I went to pitch the idea to Christine Gassman, who worked in the Process Change Department. Christine had transferred to Walt Disney World from Disney Consumer Products four years earlier, and I had been her mentor ever since. She was very receptive to the idea and dove into the project right away. The plan was to create a "first article" and then expand to additional locations depending on results. Christine got Industrial Engineering in the loop to evaluate the cost and feasibility. Eventually, we brought in Food & Beverage and Merchandise, as well as a third-party company familiar with the technology.

The first phase of the project involved installing sensors able to read the labels on the empty pallets. At any given time, the team monitoring the sensors could find out how many pallets were stacked and their precise location. Unfortunately, I left Disney before the complete implementation of the project, but to me, it highlights how partnering and collaborating can and should play out.

My point here is that all the people and departments I reached out to were quick to offer their opinion, their support, and their resources because I had established a relationship with them *before* reaching out for help.

The "Them" Syndrome

Since the dawn of humankind, there has been an "us" and a "them," whether it was the tribe across the valley, the people on the other side of the border, or the competition across the street. Nowadays, it often turns out to be the department across the hallway. The "them" group has different competencies, *raisons d'etre* and, more importantly, motives. Influenced by thousands of years of evolution, we tend to be wary of differences. Understandably, people would rather interact with individuals with whom they can easily relate. So establishing trust between not only two but several groups of people with different perspectives, approaches, and interests can be challenging.

I personally relish that challenge.

I've always looked forward to partnering and collaborating in my job. As I've shared, I am a people person. I also recognize the fact that without partners, I cannot achieve the goals I have set for myself or my organization. So there is admittedly a lot of self-interest involved. At Disney, we couldn't accomplish anything without the input of a multitude of departments. We truly needed the expertise, skills, and the perspective of a variety of players.

Here is my advice on overcoming the "them" syndrome.

First of all, find out who "they" are and, more importantly, how you can engage "them" to help you run your business better. When I was promoted to a new job, I would make a list of every department contributing to the success of my organization. I would meet the leader of every one of those departments, learn what they did, how they did it, and how we could mutually help each other. In other words, I would create a relationship with them. I would invite them to lunch or meet them in their office. Much like I did with my direct reports, I would get to know them on a personal level, find out what kept them up at night and what challenges they were facing. We would discuss how they could help my area, and how I could be the best partner for them. I would then make sure to check in on them once a quarter in person or by phone. By keeping these relationships strong, I found three areas of benefit:

Since I was interested in their work, they were more likely to think of me as a partner when they were making decisions. Top-of-mind awareness ensured they would always bring me into the loop if something were to impact my park or hotel.

Secondly, I was able to learn about areas of the business to which I had never been exposed: Industrial Engineering, Textile Services, Yield Management, Legal, Revenue Management, Labor Relations, and IT, among many others. Subsequently, I was well aware of how my department impacted their operations and would take that into consideration when making decisions.

Last but not least, when there was a new initiative, error, or crisis, we could deal with each other in a candid and transparent way. When you already know someone, you can be much more forward and upfront about your thoughts and need not worry about offending them. With the pallet initiative at the Magic Kingdom, I was comfortable submitting what could have been a flawed idea to Christine because I knew she would give me candid feedback. Had it been a bad idea, there is no doubt in my mind she would have let me know right away. Because of the trust we had established, I knew I was going to get constructive advice. Relationships grease the wheels of communication and understanding.

What areas in your company or even external contractors are key to your success? Meet them, know them, and appreciate them.

I also adhered to some basic rules of engagement when collaborating with other departments or organizations.

Engage others with an open mind. Some leaders are reluctant to collaborate because they want to retain the credit and reap all the praise of a new idea or initiative. Since nothing gets done alone, there is no rationale in being afraid of someone stealing your thunder.

Whenever we could not agree on a decision, we had to remind ourselves of what we had in common: our collectively desired outcome. Often, as divergence happens, we drift away from what we are trying to accomplish. At Disney, we always found it beneficial to consider how our decisions would impact the guests or the cast members. Neither one cared much about our department's politics or our organization's idiosyncrasies.

So get back on track, and find a happy compromise.

When there was an issue, I tried to focus on the solution and waste little time on finger-pointing. Having a post-rollout debrief session is usually when we can extract learnings from our mistakes. And remember, if you learn something from a failure, it isn't a loss.

I also always tried to project a positive, can-do attitude even in the midst of challenges. We all have our own mountain to climb. Don't be suspicious of others—just assume they have good intentions, and be quick to recognize everyone's contribution and successes.

Set the example for your organization. Encourage teams to forge relationships with other departments, too. Most of all, never let anyone denigrate or disparage another department's contribution. Remember, at the end of the day, we are all pieces of the same puzzle!

"If you want to go fast, go alone. If you want to go far, go together." —African proverb

---

Fast Track to Results

Be a great partner and foster collaboration through these approaches:

- Find out who "they" are. Look at your areas of responsibilities, and understand all the connections to the other departments that help make yours successful.
- Be proactive about meeting with your partners. For example, schedule a quarterly phone call or walk of your area to stay connected with them. Even if you do not have specific work to talk to them about, you will invariably learn something new or stumble upon new opportunity. In any case, you will be keeping the relationship "warm" for the day you do need help.
- Ask about your partners' goals. How can you help them be successful?
- When facing disagreement, rally around the shared objectives.

Part 4:

LEADING CHANGE

I n 2015, Walt Disney World underwent a large organizational change—not easy when it impacts a couple thousand leaders, but necessary and healthy in this age of disruption. The rationale behind the decision was to become more streamlined, bring about greater accountability, and give leaders exposure to new business. With this new structure, we were hoping to develop more generalists who would be better prepared to move up into executive positions. The executive team of park VPs worked on this reorganization for nine months, brainstorming several reiterations of potential structures. We looked at scope of responsibilities, reporting relationships, number of direct reports, numbers of layers, and labor savings, among other factors. We ended up eliminating an entire level of reporting (Operations Managers). We also gave general managers (who had been confined to a line of business) responsibilities for geographical areas that included Merchandise, Food & Beverage, Custodial, and attractions. Meanwhile, many leaders were changing work locations and hopping from one side of Walt Disney World to the other.

So we elaborated a plan of attack, or should I say a communication plan. We collectively decided to gather all the general managers (about fifty people) into one of our conference rooms, announced the new structure, and immediately thereafter had individual conversations with each of them. We asked the GMs to immediately inform their team leaders (now called proprietors) and have individual conversations with each and every one of them, letting them know whether they were staying or moving to another area.

This was a big day for us, and ironically, as luck would have it, I was hospitalized that very morning with acute appendicitis! No matter. My leader Jim, the senior VP of Operations, stepped into my shoes and informed my team. It was important to not miss a beat. We wanted the communication to go as quickly as possible to eliminate the anxiety-fueled conversations and speculation at the coffee machine.

During the course of one day, our entire upper management structure changed. Through it all, we made sure everyone understood the "why" behind the change. I took it one step further. Throughout the following week, I made a point of sitting in on each of the GM meetings with individual staff members to explain why they had been selected for that very position. The conversations went like this:

"Deb is now your leader in Tomorrowland. She comes to us with a proven record of being a dynamic and energetic leader, and she has the ability to think big and influence the organization. She will bring a new way of thinking about our business as she relies on her past experience in support departments ..."

"Ellen, you are now the proprietor of Tomorrowland Merchandise, where you have in-depth expertise. Since Merchandise is a new department for Deb, you will be able to teach her the intricacies of retail and help her get familiar with this new line of business ..."

"Ricky, you are now the proprietor of Cosmic Ray's. I know you have past experience in running big Food & Beverage locations. This is the busiest counter-service restaurant at Walt Disney World, and I am confident you will bring your proven experience to help us grow the business further ..."

"Melissa, you are now the Custodial proprietor in Tomorrowland. Since you excel in building relationships, we will need your skills to make sure the cast is on board as we test a new technology in your area ..."

It was important to me that everyone started their new role knowing not only why I selected them for that position but also that I had confidence they could grow the business going forward.

Considering the scope of the organizational change and how quickly we implemented it, things went rather smoothly, a testament to the adaptability of Disney leaders. The guests were none the wiser as this had no impact on the operation. If anything, it enhanced their experience as the new structure allowed a more cohesive way of running a geographic area. It's just one example of leading change through dedicated, thoughtful principles.

Chapter 18

Continuous Improvement

When your company founder is someone like Walt Disney, you know that continuous improvement will be in your organization's DNA. Walt always challenged the status quo and did not hesitate to start an entire project anew if he thought there was a better, newer, or more effective approach.

When Technicolor cameras became available in 1932, *Flowers and Trees* was already in production in black and white. No matter, Walt restarted it to integrate the latest technology in color. When trash cans did not meet his standards (the mesh cans used at the time were smelly and unattractive eyesores), he designed a new trash can with a lid and adjoining flaps. Wherever he looked, he saw room for improvement and was willing to change the way business was being done. Ever since, Walt's quest for continuous improvement has been ingrained in the Disney organization.

Part of my job as a Disney leader was to identify opportunities for better efficiency and growth. In early 1999, at Epcot, I was in charge of opening and running Test Track as the Operations manager. This new thrill ride would simulate the testing procedures General Motors used to evaluate concept cars. We initially encountered many difficulties with the new technology, and the ride would often break down.

Guests were understandably disappointed when they could not experience this new attraction. So, when Test Track was working, we looked for ways to maximize its hourly "throughput," making sure as many guests as possible could experience the ride. The vehicles accommodate six people, and most guests would show up as a party of two or more. If we were lucky, we could fill each car entirely with one party of six or a combo of several groups. When it did not add up to six people, the vehicle would be dispatched with open seats, a waste of capacity.

As we looked for ways to run the attraction at full capacity, we came up with the single riders idea. Why not have a separate line for these single riders? These guests, we envisioned, would be willing to fill the gaps on a vehicle, reducing their wait time and simultaneously increasing our hourly capacity. We presented the idea to the cast members, explained the rationale behind it, and trained them with the new loading process. The implementation was an immediate success. Soon we scaled this to the entire organization, and single-rider lines are now a legitimate part of our new-attraction queue designs.

Developing a culture of continuous improvement is contingent on your ability as a leader to create the right environment where ideas can be shared, vetted, and tested.

Give your employees a voice.

Sometimes improvement stems out of necessity. Other times, it is sheer happenstance. But more often than not, ideas emanate from the employees who are on the frontline.

As general manager of Merchandise for the Magic Kingdom, I oversaw the stroller rental location at the entrance of the park. This shop was usually slammed between 9 and 11 A.M., when most guests entered the park. We were always looking for ways to expedite the stroller rental process. One of our frontline cast members approached us one day with a simple idea: much like guests have the ability to purchase multi-day park tickets, why shouldn't we sell multi-day stroller rental passes? The guests who chose this option could simply walk to the stroller rental shop, flash their multi-day rental pass, pick a stroller, and be on their way. We all thought it was a great idea and implemented it right away. We made sure the cast member was recognized and thanked personally by all the leaders, including me. My team shared the story with all the other cast members during "Team Talks" to encourage them to share their ideas, too.

Organizations often confine employees' suggestions to an idea box somewhere in their operation. I found that giving people an opportunity to defend their ideas and rationale in person and receive recognition directly is a lot more rewarding to them. Besides, you want to make sure you thoroughly understand their ideas for improvement as it can involve aspects of the operation unfamiliar to you. Sometimes an idea solves a problem you are unaware of simply because you are not in their shoes.

When you are reviewing a suggestion, have a full discussion on the pros and cons of the idea, and then push even further. Ask the team why it may be a bad idea, why won't it work, why will it fail. By giving everyone permission to be negative, you will find chinks in the armor. You will either not move forward because of new discoveries, or make the idea even better by addressing the weaknesses.

Leaders who stay approachable and accessible will find their frontline employees walking up and supplying endless suggestions for continuous improvement. Some ideas may work; some may not be viable. Regardless, always explain your rationale and thank them for their input.

Give your employees the right resources.

If you truly want to create a culture of continuous improvement in your organization, put your money where your mouth is. In other words, be prepared to support new ideas with the right resources, be it time, labor, or money. As VP of the Magic Kingdom, I always kept a continuous improvement fund allowing us to test out ideas rapidly and on a small scale. If the idea had merit, I would look for additional resources. All my direct reports knew they had the authority to try new things and that I trusted them to make the right decisions.

In big organizations like Disney, it can be risky to implement new initiatives, so make sure you test it first. Start small with limited impact, and monitor the results. If positive, you can scale it to larger areas of your organization.

Involve all the stakeholders.

By involving all the stakeholders—no matter the job title—in the evaluation of a process or idea, leaders can gain a much clearer picture of the outcome and the most efficient way to get there. I found that when all the stakeholders take part in elaborating a new, improved process, they will more willingly adopt it or enhance it because they had the opportunity to submit their input.

With your desired outcome and stakeholder input in mind, you should immediately see where change is warranted. Resist the urge to change things just because of a new technology or because you want to leave your stamp on an organization. Implement the changes that make sense and align with your goals. Continuous improvement is not growth if it does not get you closer to achieving your vision.

Question the processes.

Let me share a common story that highlights the importance of questioning processes. A married couple is in the kitchen. The husband sits at the table reading the newspaper while the wife prepares a ham for dinner, cutting precisely one inch from either end. He questions her preparation, proclaiming, "That's a waste of good ham!"

She answers, "That's the way my mom has always prepared the ham." The husband asks why, and the wife doesn't know. Later on, she calls her mom to find out.

Her mom answers, "Because that was the way my mom, your grandma, prepared ham."

Grandma passed away several years earlier, but Grandpa is still alive. So the wife calls him to ask, "Grandpa, why did Grandma cut off one inch on either end of the ham?" He is silent as he thinks for a moment.

Then he replies, "So the ham could fit in the baking pan!"

In your organization, how many procedures are now outdated or obsolete much like the baked ham cooking process? Which steps are considered a total waste of time, and yet employees continue to execute mindlessly? If Disney is an example of most companies, the answer is a lot! Some processes are just ingrained in your organization's DNA, and no one would think of questioning why things are done that way.

Here is how to approach this: create a review process. If you have communicated a clear vision and common purpose for your team, and if you have implemented a set of quality standards permeating your entire organization, bringing consistency to decision-making, then you should be able to evaluate your processes through the same lens. For example: Does this pass the litmus test of Safety, Courtesy, Show, and Efficiency? Is it detrimental to our ability to deliver magic? How are guests affected by this process?" All good questions to ask. When we initially implemented My Magic Plus, some guests had to enter a 16-digit code to activate their band and connect it to their park tickets—how magical was that?! We quickly added a scan function to make the process easier. It is important to challenge the status quo by aligning your processes with the vision, purpose, and quality standards of your organization.

Fast Track to Results

Develop a culture of continuous improvement with these tactics:

- Experience your product or service from a customer point of view on a regular basis.
- Dedicate time to continuous-improvement events. Create roundtable opportunities to ask your team how they could improve the customer experience. Ask, "If you were in my job, what would you focus on?" It is an indirect way to solicit ideas and suggestions.
- Read customer feedback to find improvement opportunities in service and processes in your organization.
- Bring in experts and nonexperts alike into your improvement discussions. Both points of view are valuable.

Chapter 19

Bringing Change

hy are we reluctant to change?

Change is scary, difficult, and uncomfortable, as I know firsthand. I have turned my world upside down during the past two years. I went from working at a Fortune 500 company to being an entrepreneur; from leading 12,000 cast members to a grand party of one; from being responsible for a 24/7 and 365-day-per-year operation to having the most flexible work schedule ... heck, I am even moving across the country to an entirely different environment! Change can bring about many sleepless nights and much anxiety.

And in spite of all this, or possibly *because* of all this, change is also rewarding, revealing, and exhilarating. Through it all, I have learned a ton and revelled in discovering how adaptable I can be. It is now extremely gratifying to look at how far I have come, and I cannot wait to see what the future has to bring.

Still, we're wired to resist change for two major reasons: the fear of losing something we value and not knowing what awaits on the other end. Both issues should and can be alleviated to make the transition easier.

"Are you playing to win, or are you playing to not lose?"

What can you rely on?

When I decided to reorganize my entire life, I first focused on what was *not* going to change: my health, my family, my values, my knowledge, and my experience. Contemplating this gave me comfort in knowing I could always fall back on these foundational blocks of my life.

Likewise, when we bring change to a group or an organization, it is important to let people affected by change know what is *not* changing—where they can find comfort and what they can rely on. It may be the company values, culture, mission, processes, or common purpose. Employees will need an anchor to steady themselves during what can be turbulent times. They should also be able to draw comfort and reassurance from their leader. This is the support that makes change a less painful experience.

As leaders bringing change, we must go into hyper care: increase our availability and presence; increase communication and transparency; be supportive; and encourage our team members to share their experiences, learnings, and best practices. While implementing the new structure at Walt Disney World, I spent a lot of time providing that support. I emphasized how much they were learning and how valuable it was, and cheered them on along the way. I asked my GMs to share their weekly updates to me with the rest of the team so they could learn from each other. They shared their best practices and challenges as they negotiated the learning curve. And then we celebrated the milestones they reached and the accomplishments they made, even the baby steps.

I also steered team members toward the most consequential areas of their responsibilities and made sure they were applying themselves where they could create the most value. I suggested key people in support departments they could rely on for advice. With the organization changing, it was important the team found comfort in knowing that my support to them was unconditional and that they had the resources to help them succeed. Providing individuals with a reliable base, emotional support, necessary resources, and "go-to people" for expertise makes change easier and gives them the confidence they need in challenging times.

Focus on the bright side.

Obviously, you are implementing change for the better of your organization. You are looking to enhance your org chart, product, process, or strategy (or all of the above). So let your team know *why* you are going down that path, and emphasize the positive outcomes. Successful change is conditional on adopting and fostering open minds. (Much of that stems from the growth mindset I described in Chapter 2). This goes back to your ability as a leader to paint a vivid picture of what a better future looks like.

As I left Disney, I envisioned all the positive enhancement to my life: independent decision-making, flexible work hours, and the ability to travel and interact with people of various backgrounds. Granted, I was taking a calculated risk. Valerie reminded me that now that the kids were grown, we were ready to downsize and move just about anywhere in the world. And more importantly, if it did not work out, I could always go back to work for an organization and leverage twenty-six years of Disney experience. But I was mostly excited about working independently and learning new skills: marketing myself, negotiating, and accounting (yes, accounting), among others. This gave me strength and motivation.

Going back to working with my team on the reorg: I encouraged them to look at the potential learnings and positives of the experience.

I found that explaining the "why" behind decisions helped them understand, internalize, and embrace the change. Once employees know why change is happening, it is easier for them to take ownership and implement the new process, strategy, or organizational structure.

Sometimes the change isn't good news for the team. There is no way you can spin this into a positive message, and you have to implement it anyway. In these cases, you have to be up front with the team or they will see right through you. More times than I care to remember, I found myself announcing to my direct reports that we had to cut labor before the end of the fiscal year. As much as I resented doing it, it was a nonnegotiable. So the best approach was to lay it out there, explain the reasoning with as much transparency as possible, and tell my team I would fully support them through the process—and let's get it done.

Communicate the why, when, and how.

During change, nothing matters more than the quality of your communication. It is obviously an important step in change management but also something that we woefully ignore and underestimate constantly.

As I described earlier, it is best to make it as efficient as possible to eliminate angst and speculation. Be clear, be candid, be thorough, and involve all people impacted.

Take time to explain the reasoning behind your decision for change. When we understand why it is happening, we are less likely to see change as a challenge.

Make sure you are prepared to answer questions. In our case, we even had FAQs prepared in anticipation of what was bound to come up.

Your communication needs to be consistent. When we rolled out the new structure, we had a clear script to ensure consistency in our messages. The talking points were the same for all areas of the park and we shared them with the frontline leaders so they could, in turn, use them during their team talk with the frontline employees.

Well-prepared, proactive communication not only alleviates the learning curve but is also a sign of respect. You want your employees to know what is happening and why because you recognize the value they bring to the organization. It reinforces the idea of a team working toward a common purpose.

Know what to expect.

Not everybody will jump on the train immediately. Aside from a minority of enthusiasts, you will probably find the vast majority of employees are dubious at best. They are what I call the fence-sitters. They will adopt a wait-and-see approach, taking time to internalize—and this is okay. You may have been working on this novel idea or initiative for months, but they are only hearing it for the first time. So give them the "gift of time." Meanwhile, your enthusiasts will drive the train, and you can rely on them to gradually win over your fence-sitters.

Unfortunately, there will be the outright objectors, too, who will resist converting to the new process or the new structure. They resist for a plethora of reasons: they have always done it this way, and in their mind, it worked just fine; they are losing their expertise; or it threatens their control. Though the objectors are usually a minority (20% at most), we, as leaders, tend to focus on them. The truth is they will only change if *they* decide to. While we should monitor objectors so they do not poison the well, we should also avoid spending additional time and resources on them. Eventually, they will get on board or go find their happiness somewhere else.

"Change is the law of life," said John F. Kennedy, and this is even truer today. Everything around us is changing at such a rate that we can barely keep up. Bob Iger (CEO of Disney) said he devotes 30% of his time thinking about disruption. Since there is no avoiding it, we might as well embrace it and prepare for it. Fear of change is too often limiting our career and our abilities. Instead, think of it as an upgrade to a better version of yourself, your team, or your organization.

"It is not the strongest of the species that survives, nor the most intelligent that survives. It is the one that is most adaptable to change." —Charles Darwin

Fast Track to Results

Remember these tips when bringing change to an organization:

- Take time to think about everything you can rely on and will not change.
- Learn to be an optimist. These stressful times are an opportunity for us to grow and get stronger. Make a list each week of what you have learned and can apply in the future.
- As a leader, do not retreat and focus inward. Schedule time daily with your people, and be visible and approachable. These can be morning and afternoon huddles in person or by conference call. You may not have all the answers, but the power of your presence cannot be overestimated.
- Be straightforward in explaining the why behind the changes. Transparency will help win over the employees that are initially either reluctant or suspicious.

Chapter 20

Charting New Waters

I n February 2009, on my birthday no less, I was promoted from GM of Attractions at Magic Kingdom to VP of Epcot. I was both excited and nervous.

With nineteen different jobs under my belt, I have lived through quite a few learning curves while I transitioned from one role to another, but this job was a *big* one.

Fortunately, over the years, I had developed my trusted transition playbook to avoid making recurring mistakes. It is little more than a laundry list of things to think about and look out for—a checklist of the "decelerators" of a job transition. I had this playbook on my desk and reviewed it every day for the first couple of months in a new job. It helped me avoid the obvious pitfalls of being new, under stress, and trying to make a good impression.

I have always made a point of sharing these "nuggets of wisdom" with incoming new team members to let them know I had been in their shoes before. I knew what they were about to face and had learned firsthand how to avoid some of the mistakes of starting a new process or a new job.

Here are some of those pitfalls we can all avoid.

Racing to Make an Impact

The most common mistake many newly promoted leaders make is trying to prove they are worthy of their promotion. Sometimes, this translates into impulsive decisions or irrational changes. A sense of insecurity causes them to do things that may be harmful to the relationships they need to build with their new team.

I often found myself giving such leaders the same talk: "Look, you already got the job. We promoted you because we know you deserve it and we are confident you can do it." I would remind them that the cast members in their new area already knew how to do their jobs, so there was no urgency to change. Rather, the initial focus should be to create the best environment possible in which their cast could excel. Coming up with new ideas on increasing productivity was not a priority at that moment. I wrapped up by reminding them that they had a small window to make a first impression, and it had better be a good one. I suggested they personally meet with each cast member in their operation and start to create genuine interactions. Those connections and their willingness to listen and learn would later pay off big time.

Neglecting to Align Expectations

Getting some quick wins is understandable for you to build confidence and show your boss you are the right person; however, be careful to not get these quick wins at the expense of your credibility. Be sure to make sure you know what a "win" looks like before going for the score. What your vision for your department is and what your boss' vision for the department is can be very different. Take time to talk to lots of stakeholders during your transition to hear all points of view. Whatever you decide for your team and department needs to align with the rest of the organization.

Dismissing or Ignoring What You Don't Know

Our egos can get in the way of learning. We may be drawn to familiar parts of our new job because we are much more comfortable in this area. Be willing to dive into what you don't understand. Probe and learn. You have a great excuse for asking questions—you are brand-new! Asking those types of questions a year later may be problematic.

I took this exact approach when I moved to France in 1992. I was at an extremely basic level of understanding and speaking French. I decided I would take the plunge even if I had to sound fairly ridiculous stumbling through conversations. However, I had a good excuse: I had just moved there. A year later, this would not have been a viable justification. So, be humble and admit you don't know what you don't know; learn; and ask questions. People will be more inclined to help and accommodate you when you are new to the job.

Likewise, do not rely too heavily on past experience. I realize this is a hard one because our base of expertise is what we lean on every day. This is how we navigate our lives and our jobs. But when you try to learn "as a beginner," you have fresh eyes on your operation and may uncover new aspects you are not familiar with. In turn, we can avoid making assumptions and later reap valuable benefits.

Lending an Ear to a Few People

We must be careful not to pay exclusive attention to the people we naturally connect with or who are the loudest. Sometimes our opinions can become biased because we received input from a selective group or a particularly vocal person. Remember, "The squeaky wheel gets the grease." Be thoughtful to assess everyone, give everyone an opportunity to share their thoughts, and consider everyone's perspective.

Trying to Solve It All

This point goes back to an extremely important concept: the difference between problems and dilemmas. Problems have solutions: 1 + 1 = 2. I wish everything was so easy! Unfortunately, a lot of issues that are really important to us are considered dilemmas. There is no solution to dilemmas. They can only be managed. Organizational structure is a dilemma. It fits certain moments according to the business challenges, talent available, and company's objectives. It is not a permanent solution.

The day I realized that many of the issues I had been treating like problems were actually dilemmas, I took a lot of pressure off myself. Many times, there is no perfect or permanent answer! So don't think you need to bring solutions to everything because you are new.

Focusing on Process More Than People

Processes are important, but people are key to your long-term success. During my first couple of months in a job, I would do my best to meet and connect with as many people as possible and ask as many questions as I could. As I learned the operation, I would be tempted to initiate change in some of the existing processes.

Why? Because processes are a lot easier to change than people. So I would keep a notebook and write down all my observations and ideas. Once I understood the operation better, I would slowly cross off a few of my original ideas because by that point, I knew they would not work. Build relationships, rapport, and trust instead; and those relationships will reap much bigger rewards over time.

Generally, I would try not to offer my opinion unless someone asked for it. Typically, our teams expected us to make judgments and comment on our first impressions. The uninformed comments can get you in trouble. So next time you start in a new position, withhold comment until you know your operation inside and out.

Instead of falling prey to the pitfalls outlined above, leaders can chart new waters with one action.

Experiencing the Experience

"Welcome to Test Track. How many in your party?" I said again and again and again for two hours. *Right,* I thought to myself, *need to bring Courtesy to every guest.*

"Hey, Dan, I need a single!" *Right,* I thought to myself, *need to deliver Efficiency.*

"Are you guys ready for your test drive? Hold on tight!" *Right,* I thought to myself, *need to bring the Show to life.*

"Can you please tug on that seat belt for me?" *Right,* I thought to myself, *Safety comes first.* I went home that night, skipped dinner, and went straight to bed. I was exhausted.

When you start a new role at Disney, you don't just hear about and see the operations you are going to be managing—you work in them ... a lot. This was by far the most valuable time I spent early in a new job. Putting on the costume and living in the operation gave me a perspective I could never have gotten otherwise, not to mention some serious street cred. Everyone knows how important our time is, and when we choose to spend it with the people working in the trenches, the trust factor starts to rise quickly. In fact, cast members would often ask me, "Why are you wearing a costume and working with us?" The fact that they did not understand was a problem in itself. Did they not know *they* were the ones that brought the magic to life every day? Did they not understand *their performance* was the key to *my success*? Clearly, we needed to work on that message.

The other upside to working in the operation was that nobody expected me in the many meetings that would start to fill my calendar. In fact, whenever possible, I would bring in someone for the first month to run the operation, or I would deputize one of my high-performing direct reports to totally free myself up to live, eat, and breathe in the operation every day.

What you can learn when you go spend time with your people and work the trenches is priceless. Now, you may think that everyone was on their best behavior and careful about what they would say when I was around. But, magically, after a few days of seeing me showing up in costume and working side by side with them, they forgot about me as Dan the GM, or Dan the VP, and just thought about me as Dan the new employee. I started to learn which leaders were valued by the cast; which processes were dysfunctional; which tools, equipment, and supplies were lacking; what guests enjoyed and complained about—the list goes on and on. By the end of my couple of weeks of in-costume experiences, I learned more about the workings and culture of the operation than I would have over the following years, just by showing up every day and taking an interest in how things got done. So whatever is your version of working in costumes, do spend the time out there and keep your eyes and ears open. There is a wealth of information that will help guide you through a successful transition.

Many large, successful companies take the opportunity to move their people to various roles for different reasons: career development, retention, continuous improvement, and team blending. Disney is no different, and we moved people around a lot. Over the years, we talked about the advantages of moving talent but also recognized the downside to constant rotations. Training leaders in their new areas meant losing productivity during that training window. However, it is part of the growing pains and I, for one, believe that career change brings out both your true nature and true potential.

Fast Track to Results

Transition successfully in a new organization:
- Don't race to make an impact. Learn the intricacies of your organization first.

- Align your vision with the rest of the organization.
- Don't gravitate toward what you know best. Learn the ropes of what is the least familiar.
- Focus on people, all the people, not only the processes.
- Get in the trenches and work frontline positions for a while.

Chapter 21

Creativity and Innovation

hen you work for Disney, you pretty much feed off these two words. Few other organizations have committed as much time and resources to staying on the cutting edge of their industry. Past and present Disney CEOs have been dedicated to generating new content and experiences, emulating what Walt Disney himself set in motion almost 100 years ago. After taking the helm of the company, current CEO Bob Iger made some bold moves by acquiring Pixar, Lucas Films, and Marvel, thus ensuring a constant flow of new content for the organization. These very pricey bets have already paid massive dividends for Disney. And there is a whole lot more to come.

Why? Because if Disney wants guests to return, it can ill afford to grow stale. Maintaining the status quo isn't much of a strategy. The company constantly needs not only new content but also new rides, new resorts, and new experiences. And as the operation becomes more complex in the process, Disney must also innovate with the way it conducts its business. In our quickly evolving world, this is an imperative for all companies that want to stay relevant.

Here are several insights regarding creativity and innovation I have learned along the way:

Come fly with me.

Imagine you are about to fly to an unknown and far-away destination. You know it will be exotic and different; the weather will be nice and the scenery beautiful. You book your ticket and get ready for the journey. The plane takes off. You are soaring through the clouds with an open sky out the window. As you near your destination, the pilot starts the descent, lowers the landing gear, and you prepare for landing. You finally touch the tarmac, the doors open up, and the beautiful scenery appears.

This is, in my mind, a perfect analogy for the conception, evolution, and implementation of creative and innovative ideas.

First, book your ticket and get ready. In other words, invest dedicated time to creativity. Pencil in some time to generate and solicit new ideas. Since we are most creative as a group, welcome *all* the players and not only the obvious ones. Ideas come in every shape and form from all kinds of sources. Be open to listening to people from different departments, points of view, backgrounds, and industries—and why not? The very successful French cosmetic company Caudalie was created by a dermatologist who collaborated with a winemaker!

Create the right location. Most people will tell you that they think most creatively while away from their work environment. Give yourself and your team venues to be creative. Foster a conducive environment. Provide opportunities to submit ideas. At Disney, we did this through a program called "You said, we listened." Our goal was to share the great ideas submitted by employees and, more importantly, show that the leadership team was ready and willing to assist in implementing them. The ideas ranged from better bus schedules and employee cafeteria options to how to provide a new level of service to our guests. We had entire bulletin boards dedicated to this initiative, and we diligently broadcasted all the ideas that were implemented—and there were a lot of them!

Second, take to the skies. This is the "What if...?" phase of the journey. No ideas are bad or out of bounds. No judging, and no cutting—only expansion of ideas. Every suggestion should be followed by "Yes, and" instead of "No, but." This is no time for the voice of reason, rational thought, or practical remarks. Let the creative juices and imagination flow. Even if someone submits a half-baked idea, they may be onto something. Your response should be, "Tell me more." Think about where "What if...?" statements lead to. "What if every car could be a taxi?" led to the creation of ridesharing companies Uber and Lyft. "What if every room could be a hotel?" led to Airbnb. "What if guests could make a reservation for an attraction?" led to Disney's FastPass. "What if we could create a real safari in Florida?" led to the construction of Kilimanjaro Safaris at Animal Kingdom.

Each one of these initial pitches seemed crazy and had no precedent; conventional wisdom would say that it was too hard, too complex, or could not be done.

Third, prepare for landing and get back to the ground. This is when imagination and creativity take shape and become innovation. Once the ideas have had a chance to emerge, brew, and stew, it is time for practicality, adaptation, and implementation. Be ready to ask a lot of questions. "Do we have the resources? Personnel? Technology? Time? Money? Knowledge? Talent? Which obstacles are we bound to encounter?" And my all-time favorite: "Why won't this work?" This is a valid question. If answered honestly, potential roadblocks and pitfalls will emerge and get ironed out before they become an issue. It is important to not shut down suggestions too quickly during the landing—but critical thinking is allowed to weed out unrealistic ideas.

Ideally, by now you have reached your destination. The doors open to a brand-new process, project, product, and strategy—and you can look forward to an improved version of your business.

"The future belongs to those who see possibilities before they become obvious." —John Sculley

---

Not all great ideas are big ideas.

During my years at Disney, I witnessed its creativity and innovative talent expand into new cities (Paris, Hong Kong, Shanghai) and new industries (cruise lines, timeshares); and bring new technology to the theme-park business (Disney My Magic Plus). These are what I like to call the Big, Hairy, and Audacious Ideas—the ones that take an entire organization's time and resources to bring to life. But I am not talking exclusively about the mega projects or revolutionary products; I am also talking about the need to be creative and innovative at all levels of an organization regardless of the scope of the initiative. Sometimes, it is simply about problem-solving.

Here is a modest example: at 9 a.m., as Magic Kingdom opened, I could see families come pouring down the main entrance aiming for their first ride of the day. As they passed the Main Street Starbucks, adult guests jockeyed for one last cup of coffee before facing the day. But the line could be pretty long in the early morning, and time was of the essence—the kids were eager to hit their favorite attraction. How could we make it easier on them? How about an express line for Pike Place brewed coffee only? No fancy lattes or macchiatos, just one simple cup of java. In and out in under 60 seconds. The Food and Beverage team solved the problem by running a small pop-up coffee station in front of Starbucks, equipped with handheld credit card devices, and a setup simple enough to be broken down at the end of the morning rush. Coffee sales went up, the adults got their caffeine, and kids were happily trotting toward their first ride.

Admittedly, this idea was not the caliber of new attractions or bleeding-edge technology, but it was still creative, and it solved a problem. How many of these opportunities are out there? More than you could ever hope to solve in a career. It's a target-rich environment! These problems may not be as dramatic, and the solutions may not cost millions of dollars, but that does not change the fact that they require thinking out of the box. More often than not, these suggestions will emanate from the frontline team members who know the inside of the organization, which brings me to my next point…

Nobody has a monopoly on creativity.

At Disney, we were lucky enough to have an entire department devoted to all things creative. Whether we were building a new store, attraction, park, or resort; upgrading hotel rooms or restaurants; changing cast members' costumes, or simply repainting, the approval and creative process inevitably went through WDI, Walt Disney Imagineering.

For most of my career, Disney expected operators like me to focus on executing the plan while giving the WDI team the monopoly and control on creativity. Fortunately, things have been changing as of late—for the better, I should add. There is now a much-needed collaboration between the Design teams and the Operations teams.

Creativity and innovation should not be exclusive to a specific category of people with specific qualifications. *Unlikely* people have *accidentally* created a lot of the best inventions. And Disney employees have incredibly creative ideas, which were found in unexpected situations, such as when Custodial cast members started drawing Mickey Mouse faces with a broom and water to entertain our guests. Or when housekeepers creatively folded towels into animals and surprised young hotel guests who would find them on their hotel beds. Not to mention all the themed food items over time, from chocolate Cinderella slippers to Star Wars cupcakes; all ideas brought forth by frontline cast members at a minimal cost. And when it comes to creative problem-solving, no one is better equipped than the people who deal with the issue day in, day out.

What are we solving for?

At one point, we thought it would be good for Walt Disney World to have a "talking" Mickey. A collaborative team of both WDI and Entertainment worked on the project, dedicating a lot of resources to this initiative. We decided to test it out at the Magic Kingdom before rolling it out to the rest of Walt Disney World. The "enhanced" Mickey worked well enough, but we quickly saw it had little impact on the guest experience. The ratings were no different whether Mickey was able to talk or not. In fact, most of our guests believed Mickey had always been talking anyway!

The learning here was twofold. First, what you consider an issue may not be one for your customers. So stay tuned to what they want before launching a new initiative.

The second: when trying to problem solve, always keep track of what the issue is. Had we asked ourselves, "What are we trying to solve?" we would have realized that it was a nonissue. Sometimes, our thirst for creativity and innovation just gets us carried away.

Fast Track to Results

Creativity and innovation will sprout from these initiatives:
- Brainstorming in a nontraditional, comfortable place for the group, off property if possible.
- Interactive games or activities to get participants in the right mindset.

- "What if…" questions to find creative solutions for the issues at hand. (What if we did not have offices? What if we only had one meeting a week? What if our customers could name their own price?)
- A notetaker to capture all ideas, and recap it after the meeting to determine next steps.
- The "sky's the limit" part of the brainstorming, where everyone builds onto everyone else's ideas without judgment or limits.
- The "let's come down to earth" part of the brainstorming, where everyone starts to evaluate the actual potential, resources, and needs to implement good ideas.

Conclusion

*O*n a recent trip to Japan, I visited the Zen garden at Ryōan-ji Temple in Kyoto. I spent quite a bit of time there, and I soon realized this interesting sight perfectly encapsulated how I think about leadership and what matters most. Hear me out.

This 2,600-square-foot dry garden includes fifteen stones carefully placed in white gravel in groups of two, three, or five. First of all, all the stones of the garden have different sizes, shapes, and colors and are placed strategically to showcase their best side. Likewise, in your organization, you need to surround yourself with a diverse team that brings different talents to complement your own. Each individual needs to be in an environment where they can shine and leverage their skills and potential. Only then can you move forward individually *and* as a team.

Secondly, Ryōan-ji garden is a marvel of simplicity. The clean lines, perfectly raked gravel, and plain background make it an ideal place to meditate. When things are clear and straightforward, mindfulness is within reach. *Clarity unlocks potential.* With a clear goal, you as a leader can lead yourself and your team more efficiently; you have a greater impact on your organization, and you can lead effectively through change. Your success as a leader is contingent on your ability to develop clear goals for yourself and everyone around you.

Last but not least, the particularity of this dry garden is the fact that the fifteen stones have been carefully placed in such a way that the composition *can never be seen in its entirety* from the viewing platform. Regardless of where you stand, you will be able to account for fourteen of the stones, but never will all fifteen be visible from any given spot. No one knows for sure of the meaning behind the designer's intent, and many interpretations have been debated throughout the years. I personally believe there is a hidden message in the layout: the blind spot.

Life is full of things we don't know; things we are not aware of; things we can't anticipate or prepare for; or things we simply choose to ignore; our blind spot. This makes us vulnerable and prone to errors. It sometimes leads us to irrational decisions or assumptions.

You can only prevent this blind spot with help. At Ryōan-ji, when partners stand on the platform with you, staring at the same garden, you collectively cover *the blind spot*. As a group, it becomes possible to account for all the stones, much like teamwork allows you to foresee and avoid roadblocks and challenges.

This is why I believe relationships are so important. Your work environment is a reflection of the quality of the relationships you maintain with your team; better yet, relationships are the *foundation of your organization's culture*. They pave the way to engagement and commitment. With great relationships, there is trust. Where there is trust, there is empowerment. Where there is empowerment, there is ownership. Where there is ownership, there is motivation. Where there is motivation, there is creativity—and risk-taking, and problem-solving, and resilience, and ultimately success. This is what a great culture can do for your kingdom!

Acknowledgments

Mom, thank you for your empathy and counsel in navigating life professionally and personally.

Dad, thank you for your advice and wisdom, which have given me the confidence to lead a life I could have never imagined.

Jullian, Margot, and Tristan, parents sometimes wonder what kind of legacy they will leave for their children. Your grandparents started the journey for your mother and me, and we have done our best to help you prepare for your adventure as you become young adults. We are so proud of who you have become and are excited to watch you grow. We will always be there for you.

Valerie, my sweet wife and brilliant editor. Thank you for supporting and accompanying me on this exciting journey. Without you, it would mean nothing.

And, last but not least, Nick, Sarah, Jennifer, and the team at Morgan James Publishing, thank you for the magic that pulled all the pieces together we needed to bring this book to life.

About the Author

Dan attended Boston University, graduating in 1991, where he earned a Bachelor of Arts degree in Political Science. An avid rugby player, he was selected for the 1990 and 1991 USA Collegiate All-American Rugby team and was Captain for the 1991 team.

Upon graduation from Boston University in 1991, Dan moved to Florida and worked as a parking attendant at Disney's Epcot Center. Subsequently, he joined the Disneyland Paris Management Trainee Program, as part of the opening team.

While in France, he held various management positions in Park Operations. He and his wife Valerie, who was also with Disneyland Paris, were married in France and spent five years there before moving back to Orlando in 1997.

Since that time, Dan has held various executive operations roles at the Walt Disney World Resort, both in the theme parks and resort hotels, and retired as the Vice President of the Magic Kingdom where he led 12,000 cast members and entertained over 20 million guests annually.

He earned his MBA in 2001 at the Crummer School of Business at Rollins College. In addition to his operational responsibilities, Dan was a keynote speaker for the world-renowned Disney Institute for 18 years. He has addressed open-enrollment participants as well as attendees in customized programs including the USAA Bank, General Motors, the U.S. Department of State, the U.S. Army, the Southern Methodist University Business School, Porsche A.G., and United Airlines.

He served on the board of Junior Achievement of Central Florida from 2004 to 2018, and was Chairman in 2010.

After a fulfilling and exciting 26-year career with the Walt Disney Company, Dan and Valerie made the decision to set out on a new venture and start their own consulting and speaking business.

Dan and Valerie provide customized, authentic presentations focusing on leadership and management practices, drawing upon their extensive Disney career with relevant examples and inspiring storytelling.